Lewis and Clark's Journey of Discovery in American History

Other titles *in American History*

The Alamo
in American History
(ISBN 0-89490-770-0)

Alcatraz Prison
in American History
(ISBN 0-89490-990-8)

The Battle of the Little Bighorn
in American History
(ISBN 0-89490-768-9)

The Boston Tea Party
in American History
(ISBN 0-7660-1139-9)

The California Gold Rush
in American History
(ISBN 0-89490-878-2)

The Fight for Women's
Right to Vote
in American History
(ISBN 0-89490-986-X)

The Great Depression
in American History
(ISBN 0-89490-881-2)

The Industrial Revolution
in American History
(ISBN 0-89490-985-1)

Japanese-American Internment
in American History
(ISBN 0-89490-767-0)

John Brown's Raid
on Harpers Ferry
in American History
(ISBN 0-7660-1123-2)

Latter-day Saints and
the Mormon Trail
in American History
(ISBN 0-89490-988-6)

The Lincoln Assassination
in American History
(ISBN 0-89490-886-3)

McCarthy and the Fear of
Communism in American History
(ISBN 0-89490-987-8)

Native Americans and the
Reservation in American History
(ISBN 0-89490-769-7)

The Oregon Trail
in American History
(ISBN 0-89490-771-9)

The Panama Canal
in American History
(ISBN 0-7660-1216-6)

The Salem Witchcraft Trials
in American History
(ISBN 0-7660-1125-9)

The Transcontinental Railroad
in American History
(ISBN 0-89490-882-0)

The Underground Railroad
in American History
(ISBN 0-89490-885-5)

The Watergate Scandal
in American History
(ISBN 0-89490-883-9)

IN
AMERICAN
HISTORY

LEWIS AND CLARK'S JOURNEY OF DISCOVERY IN AMERICAN HISTORY

Judith Edwards

Enslow Publishers, Inc.

40 Industrial Road   PO Box 38
Box 398   Aldershot
Berkeley Heights, NJ 07922   Hants GU12 6BP
USA   UK

http://www.enslow.com

Dedication

To Benjamin

Library of Congress Cataloging-in-Publication Data

Edwards, Judith, 1940–
    Lewis and Clark's journey of discovery in American history / Judith Edwards.
        p.   cm. — (In American history)
    Includes bibliographical references and index.
    Summary: An account of the Lewis and Clark expedition, describing its mishaps, adventures, and impact on western expansion.
    ISBN 0-7660-1127-5
    1. Lewis and Clark Expedition (1804–1806)—Juvenile literature.
    2. West (U.S.)—Discovery and exploration—Juvenile literature. [1. Lewis and Clark Expedition (1804–1806) 2. West (U.S.)—Discovery and exploration.] I. Title. II. Series.
    F592.7.E39 1999
    917.804'2—dc21   98-14484
                                                               CIP
                                                               AC

Printed in the United States of America

10 9 8 7 6 5 4 3 2

Illustration Credits: American Philosophical Society, pp. 32, 65, 108; Enslow Publishers, Inc., pp. 11, 19, 98; Independence National Historical Park, pp. 14, 17, 22; Judith Edwards, pp. 40, 66, 68, 77, 88, 111; Library of Congress, pp. 34, 56; Montana Historical Society, Helena, pp. 8, 38, 63, 72, 74, 84, 86, 100.

Cover Illustration: Independence National Historical Park; Montana Historical Society, Helena.

★ CONTENTS ★

PREPARING FOR ADVENTURE

An interesting question was now to be determined; which of these rivers was the Missouri, or that river which the Minnetares had discribed to us as approaching very near to the Columbia river. to mistake the stream . . . would not only loose us the whole of this season but would probably so dishearten the party that it might defeat the expedition altogether.[1]

—Meriwether Lewis, June 3, 1805

Two tall men dressed in moccasins and buckskin stood on a point overlooking two large rivers. They looked puzzled and were talking rapidly and pointing first to one river and then the other. Behind them, in a crude camp, were twenty-nine other bearded and buckskinned men, one woman, one baby, and a big black dog. An air of suspense loomed and there was much conversation. The date was June 3, 1805. The men pointing at the rivers were Captains Meriwether Lewis and William Clark, the leaders of this group called the Corps of Discovery. They had been traveling up the Missouri River from Wood River, Illinois, by boat and over land, since May 14, 1804. Now they had

*This is a view of the area where the Marias and Missouri
rivers meet as it looks today.*

come to a point where two large rivers intersected. If they made a mistake and followed the wrong river, it would seriously delay the expedition and discourage everyone involved.

Captain Lewis wrote about this dilemma in his journal that night. How terrible it would be to take the wrong river after traveling for more than a year on a trip that was supposed to take the expedition to the Pacific Ocean! As Lewis said, it might mean the ruin of the whole expedition, because winter would come soon. This winter would be the second one the group had spent without reaching the Pacific, and their lack of supplies might mean they would have to turn around, without achieving their goal.[2]

The Corps of Discovery had already been through many challenges. A day before the expedition camped at the fork of the two rivers, the French interpreter Toussaint Charbonneau was chased by a grizzly bear into some bushes. If not for the sharpshooting of George Drouillard, the expedition's best hunter, both men might have been killed. In April, when Captain Lewis shot the first grizzly of the trip, another bear chased him eighty yards into the river!

The threat of stumbling across angry poisonous rattlesnakes was a daily occurrence. Captain Clark was almost bitten by a rattlesnake on May 17. On May 29 the Corps of Discovery had a surprise visitor. A huge buffalo swam across the river to the camp. It was night, and only the soldier on guard duty was awake. By the time he saw the buffalo, it was running straight for the fires, galloping within inches of the heads of some of the sleeping men. The guard yelled and jumped up and down, trying to divert the attention of this immense animal. Lewis's big Newfoundland dog, Seaman, barked wildly. Finally, the confused buffalo turned to the side and disappeared as quickly as it had come. The members of the expedition were by then fully awake, guns in hand, nobody knowing what had caused the disturbance.

The weather was often cold and rainy. The Missouri River became so shallow at some points that the men had no choice but to walk on the riverbank and pull the boats along with ropes. The uniforms and shoes the men had started out with were long since worn out. The moccasins they had made did little to protect their sore feet from the rocks and prickly pear cactus plants. But for the moment, at least, there was no threat from the Teton Sioux, a fierce Indian tribe that had confronted them last fall. That incident was a narrow escape, and they hoped it would not be repeated.

Now the Corps of Discovery was faced with a decision that was just as dramatic and held great danger if the choice turned out to be wrong. The members of the expedition were sure that the river they should take was the north fork. It was wider than the other river and looked similar to the waters of the Missouri, on which they had traveled for so many painful miles. The captains, after study and exploration, became convinced that proceeding on the south fork was the correct decision. Lewis wrote,

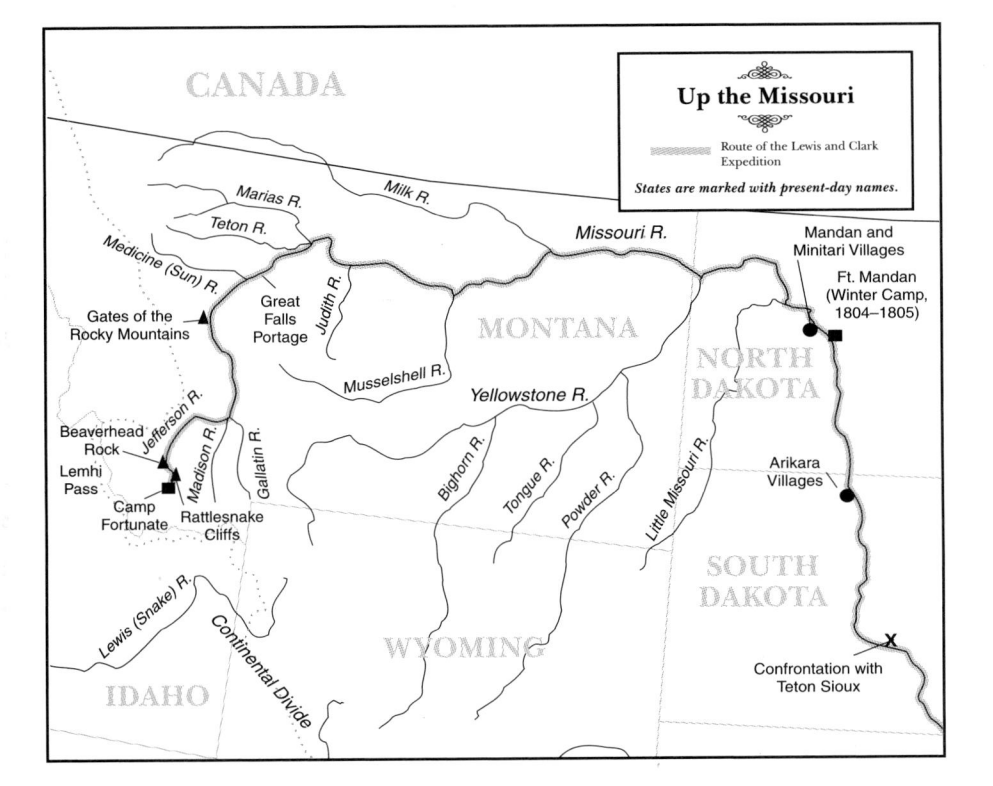

This map shows the route taken by the Lewis and Clark expedition up the Missouri River, and the area at which they had to decide which fork to follow toward the Pacific Ocean.

Those ideas as they occurred to me I indevoured to impress on the minds of all the party all of whom except Capt. C. being still firm in the belief that the N. Fork was the Missouri and that which we ought to take; they said very cheerfully that they were ready to follow us any wher we thought proper to direct but that they still thought that the other was the river. . . .[3]

Just why were these wilderness travelers so willing to follow their leaders, even when they thought their leaders were choosing the wrong river? Why were they traveling in this dangerous, uncomfortable wilderness, where around every bend lay the unexpected? Let's find out what thirty-two people, plus a baby, were doing on a riverbank near present-day Great Falls, Montana, in June 1805.

The Lewis and Clark expedition was born in the mind of Thomas Jefferson, third president of the United States. Jefferson's pioneering mind put him way ahead of his time. He was a naturalist—someone who studies the earth and its inhabitants, and a botanist—a person who studies plant life. Jefferson was also an architect, having designed

SETTING THE STAGE FOR THE EXPEDITION

his own home, Monticello, in Virginia. He was also one of the world's first archaeologists, studying civilizations and events from the past by examining buildings and tools of everyday use, which are called artifacts. Jefferson owned many articles dug up from the ruins of earlier times. Monticello is full of practical inventions and evidence of his ability to create beautiful surroundings.

Though Thomas Jefferson had traveled a great deal in Europe, in America he had never traveled more than fifty miles west of his home. He was fascinated and curious about what lay beyond the western frontier, which in those days was the territory west of the

The Lewis and Clark expedition was planned by Thomas Jefferson, shown here in a portrait by Charles Willson Peale.

Mississippi River. It was his vision that made the Lewis and Clark expedition possible by pushing forward the United States purchase of the Louisiana Territory. Thomas Jefferson knew that the fur trade with American Indians would be valuable to some country, and he wanted America to be that country. He also knew that important information about natural resources and other cultures would help the United States grow.

American hunters and trappers were crossing the Appalachian Mountains as early as 1738, even though the land west of the Mississippi River was claimed by Spain and France. These countries had explored the vast new continent of North America for many years, and they, like the United States, saw the potential for riches and expansion. However, no one had any idea of what the entire West was like, or even how much there was of it.

The Northwest Passage

Alexander Mackenzie, a brilliant and daring Canadian explorer, attempted to find a northwest route to the Pacific in 1789 and again in 1793. He wrote a book called *Voyages from Montreal, on the River St. Lawrence, Through the Continent of North America, to the Frozen and Pacific Ocean*, which was published in 1801. It was the first book that discussed and contained maps of the far Northwest. It contained much information about distances and land formations that an expedition might need. Jefferson had studied this book, and Lewis and Clark took a copy west with them.

Jefferson was aware of Canadian exploration efforts to find the Northwest Passage. He was most eager to send an expedition into the Louisiana Territory to claim it, if possible, for the United States, "for the purpose of commerce."[1] This meant he wanted to find an inland waterway for the transport of furs, the major money-making product during the first half of the nineteenth century. The country that successfully established a trade route would become very wealthy. Like many Americans before him, Jefferson hoped that the Missouri River would continue right across the continent and join with the Columbia River, which was believed to flow to the Pacific Ocean.

Meriwether Lewis was a Virginia neighbor of Jefferson's, and President Jefferson appointed Lewis to be his private secretary in 1801. Jefferson knew that Lewis was an experienced woodsman and a respected military leader. He also knew that Lewis was intelligent and hardworking. So this "private secretary" became more pupil than employee, as Jefferson taught or arranged for lessons in natural history, botany, navigation, and medicine. By the time Jefferson had appropriated funds from Congress for the western trip, twenty-nine-year-old Lewis was fully capable of leading the expedition.

This is a portrait of Meriwether Lewis, the leader of the Lewis and Clark expedition, painted by Charles Willson Peale.

The Louisiana Purchase

At first, the legality of the expedition was questionable. After all, Spain owned the territory over which the Corps of Discovery would march. And then, just as plans for outfitting the expedition got underway, Napoleon Bonaparte, the emperor of France, bought the Louisiana Territory from Spain. Napoleon was afraid that Great Britain, France's enemy, would send armies to capture Louisiana. He decided he would rather sell it to the United States than have to mount a war in far-off North America. If Napoleon had not sold this land to the United States, the Corps of Discovery would have had an even more dangerous trip—across foreign territory owned by France and Spain. However, in April 1803, Congress paid France $15 million for 828,000 square miles of uncharted territory. The Louisiana Purchase about doubled the size of the United States.

The United States was now the official owner of the Louisiana Territory and Jefferson gave his instructions to Lewis. "The object of your mission is to explore the Missouri," Jefferson said, and any other waterways that could carry travelers to the Pacific Ocean. The expedition was to map the area of the Missouri River. Lewis was to learn as much as possible about the native peoples and to be friendly to them, assuring them that the purpose of the journey was one of peace and a wish for commerce. But, Jefferson said, while being "neighborly and friendly and useful to

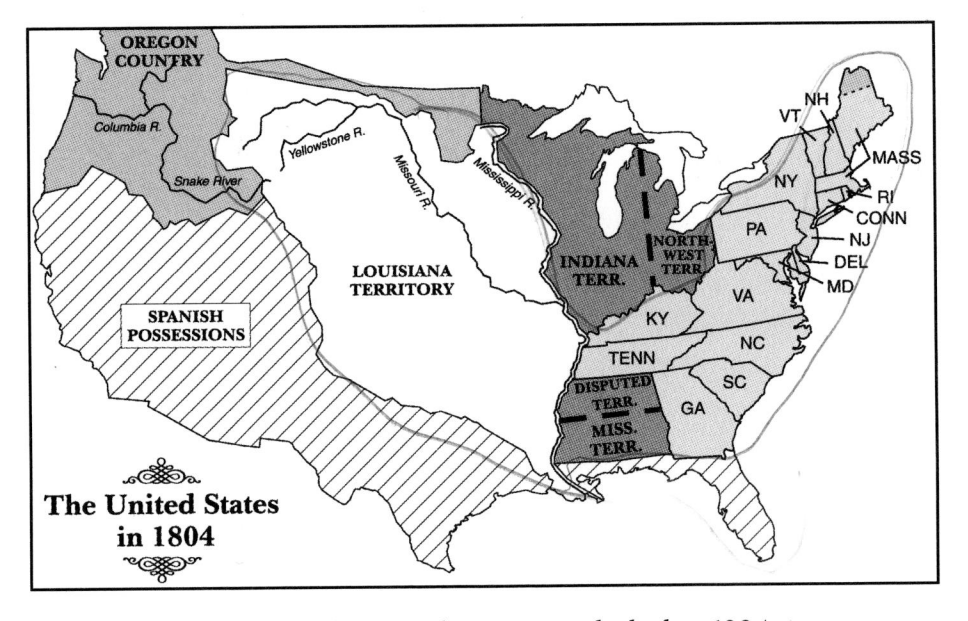

The United States
in 1804

This map shows the United States as it looked in 1804, just
after the addition of the Louisiana Territory.

them," Lewis was to be sure to impress the Indians with the power and extent of the United States.[2]

Jefferson also wanted to know about the animals, minerals, soil, and climate of the area. Lewis was to observe and record everything that would possibly be of interest to the United States, scientifically and commercially. He was to consider, on the return trip, retracing the path to double-check his observations. Jefferson and Lewis worked together to plan the details of the expedition—first of all deciding just who would be included in the Corps of Discovery.

Captains Meriwether Lewis and William Clark

William Clark, who was thirty-four years old in 1803, had served in the army with Meriwether Lewis, and they had gotten along very well. Lewis and Clark liked and respected each other.

SOURCE DOCUMENT

THE OBJECT OF YOUR MISSION IS TO EXPLORE THE MISSOURI RIVER AND SUCH PRINCIPAL STREAMS OF IT, AS BY IT'S COURSE AND COMMUNICATION WITH THE WATERS OF THE PACIFIC OCEAN, WHETHER THE COLUMBIA, OREGON, COLORADO OR ANY OTHER RIVER MAY OFFER THE MOST DIRECT & PRACTICABLE WATER COMMUNICATION ACROSS THE CONTINENT FOR THE PURPOSES OF COMMERCE.[3]

This is an excerpt from the instructions President Thomas Jefferson issued to Lewis and Clark before they began on their journey to the Pacific Coast.

The two men had very different personalities. Lewis had been specially trained for the trip and was better educated than Clark. However, Lewis was known to be moody, sometimes quiet and withdrawn. Clark was warm and outgoing, with a steady, practical nature that was a good contrast to Lewis's reserve. Like Lewis, Clark was tall, physically strong, and at home in the woods.[4]

Though Lewis put in a request to have Lieutenant Clark made a captain, that commission never came through, due to unexplained political pressures in Washington, D.C. However, the other members of the expedition never knew that. Lewis insisted that both men be referred to as captain and share totally equal leadership during the whole trip. The strong, disciplined, intelligent leadership by Lewis and Clark is the main reason the expedition was so successful. First, they had to instill discipline in the group of rugged young frontiersmen they selected for the trip.

Turning Frontiersmen into Corpsmen

When the expedition was authorized by Congress on July 2, 1803, the Corps of Discovery was to include twelve men. Dependable, strong, persevering, and unmarried men were to be recruited from the army. Hunters were on top of the list. Also desired were carpenters, ironworkers, and gunsmiths. Army discipline was to ensure a successful journey under difficult conditions. The going wage for privates in the army was five dollars a month, with an additional five dollars

This is William Clark, the co-commander of the Corps of Discovery, as painted by Charles Willson Peale.

for clothing. Lewis authorized an offer of double pay—ten dollars a month—along with automatic discharge from the army on their return, and a grant of western land for each man.

Among the corps members were men such as John Colter, a private citizen who, like all the corpsmen except for the interpreters, was required to enlist in the United States Army for the journey. Colter was later to discover the land that makes up Yellowstone Park today, and have exciting adventures of his own.[5] He was one of the best hunters and scouts of the expedition. He was also one of the first to be disciplined severely while the expedition waited to get under way—for being absent without permission and talking roughly to an officer. One of the tasks of the captains was to turn independent woodsmen into army privates with a respect for group discipline.

Private George Shannon was the youngest member of the expedition. He was just seventeen years old when he joined the Corps of Discovery. Eventually he became a lawyer and a state senator from Kentucky. On the expedition he was valued as a hunter, a horseman, and a singer! He was also lost several times on the journey, once for sixteen days.

In addition to the enlisted men and officers, the expedition took along several interpreters. George Drouillard was the son of a Shawnee woman and a French trapper. He spoke French and English and was familiar with Indian sign language. He became the major interpreter on the trip. He would prove to be calm and quick in a crisis.

Shopping for the Journey

In addition to finding suitable men to enlist for this tough journey, Lewis had to outfit the entire trip. Imagine trying to pack for a journey into unknown wilderness. The expedition would be traveling by boat, horse, and foot, and no one had any idea of how long the trip would take or even where it would lead them. They also had to be ready for encountering hostile people. Although this was a wilderness to white Americans, it was home to millions of Indians, native to the land, who might not be happy to see them.

Supplies that would last a very long time had to be made and purchased in many different locations. There was no modern equipment for cooking at campsites. Though the men were expected to hunt for their meat supply, there had to be food such as flour, salt pork, and salt. There were also 193 pounds of dried soup!

Lewis consulted with Dr. Benjamin Rush, a prominent physician who had been a signer of the Declaration of Independence. Rush advised Lewis about the importance of rest when ill (something that was to prove impossible during the expedition) and of fasting to ward off fever. He also gave Lewis his famous "Rush's pills," which Rush believed would cure almost everything. Actually, they were a powerful laxative with mercury as the main ingredient, which is known today to be poisonous. It was quite lucky that no one was killed because of those pills. Such was the state of medicine in 1803. Rush also gave Lewis a list of medical questions to ask the Indians, because nothing was known about the daily habits and diseases of the native tribes.

All medicines had to be carried with the members of the expedition, as well as rifles, gunpowder, fishhooks, knives, flints to set fires, flannel cloth, woolen overalls, candles, ink, mosquito netting, and goods for the Indians. These goods were to be traded with the Indians for food and other items and to buy friendship and show the wealth and power of the United States. There were lots of beads, thimbles, needles, thread, combs, calico, paints, and other items the native people would find fascinating. Even with all the planning, the men of the expedition had to make their clothing from animal skins quite early in the trip. The terrain and weather proved rougher than they could ever have imagined. They could only hope they had brought enough of the things that were really important— rifles, ammunition, ink, and paper.

And We're Off!

On July 4, 1803, Lewis learned through a newspaper report that his expedition would, indeed, be legal. The Louisiana Territory had officially been sold to the United States by Napoleon. Just two days earlier, Lewis had received his final letter of credit from Thomas Jefferson, authorizing expenditures for the trip. This meant Lewis could finish buying supplies and

ARTICLE I

. . . THE FIRST CONSUL OF THE FRENCH REPUBLIC DESIRING TO GIVE TO THE UNITED STATES A STRONG PROOF OF HIS FRIENDSHIP, DOTH HEREBY CEDE TO THE SAID UNITED STATES, IN THE NAME OF THE FRENCH REPUBLIC, FOREVER AND IN FULL SOVEREIGNTY, THE SAID TERRITORY [LOUISIANA], WITH ALL ITS RIGHTS AND APPURTENANCES, AS FULLY AND IN THE SAME MANNER AS THEY HAVE BEEN ACQUIRED BY THE FRENCH REPUBLIC . . .[6]

This is an excerpt from the agreement in which France sold the Louisiana Territory to the United States.

paying for equipment. He left Philadelphia for Pittsburgh to make final arrangements for the journey. All that was left was for Clark to accept Lewis's offer to be co-captain. On July 29 Clark's letter of acceptance arrived. The keelboat for the expedition was completed at the end of August, and Lewis set forth on the Ohio River, on his way to the Missouri.

By the time the expedition set out from Wood River, Illinois, in 1804, the Corps of Discovery had grown from twelve to forty-three! As Lewis planned for the trip and became more aware of all it entailed, he felt it was important to increase the number of people on the expedition.

There were "nine young men from Kentucky; 14 soldiers of the United States Army . . . two French watermen; an interpreter and hunter and a black servant belonging to Captain Clarke."[7] Seven more soldiers and nine more watermen also went along for the journey as far as the Mandan Indian villages near present-day Bismarck, North Dakota. They set out in three boats, two large rowboats called pirogues with six and seven oars each, and the large, square boat called a keelboat, with twenty-two oars! This boat was to carry supplies. It had a midsection that could be raised to make a fort if the corps were attacked. Two horses were led along the riverbank for hunting.

Also lining the bank were "many of the neighbouring inhabitents" waving good-bye and good luck as the Corps of Discovery set out from the frontier of America to travel into what was, for them, the unknown.[8]

Imagine the excitement of these young men, taking off up the wild Missouri River after a winter of drill, preparation, and boredom!

In itself, the Missouri was a major challenge. The river has long been described as wild and rough, with its own individual personality, by everyone from river travelers to geographers. From its junction with the Mississippi, above St. Louis, to its source high in the Rocky Mountains in southwestern Montana, the Missouri is 2,714 miles long, the longest river in North America. Famed for its powerful flooding and wild swings of direction, the Missouri changed course and caused many changes of landscape before man-made reservoirs at least partially controlled its natural state. Because it is largely frozen in the winter, its own melting ice added to melting snows makes it dangerously powerful. As prairie rivers join, silt is deposited, giving the Missouri the nickname Big Muddy.

Sailing the Missouri

Added to the challenge for the expedition was that the members of the Corps of Discovery soon realized

RUNNING UP THE MISSOURI

going "up" the Missouri, against the current, slowed their forward rush. These young explorers, so eager and excited to be on their way, were rowing and sailing against the often strong flow of the river trying to take them downstream. Fourteen miles a day was good progress.

Captain Clark noted that the banks of the river were composed of sand and would often tumble into the river unexpectedly.[1] Drifting logs, hurtled forward by the speed of the river, rammed the large and awkward keelboat. This shallow, covered riverboat was usually used for short freight hauls, not as the major conveyance for a long trip. An overhanging tree branch broke the mast of this floating fort. The Missouri River was showing them who was boss, just in case they did not know. They hit snags and sandbars. Often there was no wind for the sail, and the river was too swift for oars to row against. At those times, the men walked along the banks of the river, towing the keelboat with ropes.

The keelboat itself was so tightly packed with trade goods and supplies for the long trip that there was nowhere to turn around without bumping into a box or crate. Often the boat had to be repacked because it had been loaded unevenly.

But worst of all were the bugs. Gnats swarmed around the men's eyes and up their noses, but they were nothing compared with the mosquitoes. Even Captain Lewis's dog, Seaman, yowled at night because of the mosquitoes. We know just how much the expedition members hated the mosquitoes because they are mentioned in the journals in increasingly strong terms. First, the mosquitoes are called "troublesome," then, they become "very troublesome," "immensely troublesome," "exceedingly troublesome," "immensely numerous and troublesome!" But the irritation was really the least of the expedition's problems with mosquitoes. Though they did not know it at the time, mosquitoes could also be dangerous carriers of diseases such as malaria.[2]

Keeping Journals

During this time the captains, sergeants, and at least one of the privates were writing down everything they saw and experienced. If not for those journals, we would not be able to read and learn about this wonderfully exciting adventure. Even with the mud, rain, and interminable mosquitoes, Captain Lewis managed to comment on the utterly beautiful land around the unpredictable river.[3] He methodically collected new plants and animals and wrote about them in great scientific detail. The hunting was good. Wild turkey, deer, and bears were plentiful. Snakes were another thing altogether, and Private Joseph Field became severely ill from a snakebite.

The first July 4 was spent dancing to expedition member Pierre Cruzatte's fiddle and shooting off the keelboat's big gun near creeks the corps members named Fourth of July Creek and Independence Creek. Partying aside, the grueling work and uncomfortable

of small fish which now begin to run and are
taken in great quantities in the Columbia R.
about 40 miles above us by means of skiming
or scooping nets. on this page I have drawn
the likeness of them as large as life; it
as perfect as I can make it with my
pen and will serve to give a
general idea of the fish. the
rays of the fins are boney but
not sharp tho somewhat pointed.
the small fin on the back
next to the tail has no
rays of bone being a
bananous pellicle.
to the gills have
each. those of the
eight each, thos
are 20 and 2
that of the back
the fins are of
is of a bluish
the the lower
is of a silve-
part. the
behind the
second of
the purple
a silve
and
like

thin mes
the fins an
eleven rays
abdomen have
of the pinnoan
half formed in fron
has eleven rays. all
a white colour. the bac
duskey colour and that of
part of the sides and belly
-ng white. no spots on any
first bone of the gills nex
eye is of a bluis cast, and the
a light goald colour nearly whit
of the eye is black and the iris of
white. the under jaw exceeds the upe
the mouth opens to great extent, foldin
that of the herring. it has no teeth.
the abdomen is obtuse and smooth; in this
differing from the herring, shad anchovey;
&c of the Malacapterygious Order & Class
Clupea

Lewis and Clark made extremely detailed notes of the sights and sounds they experienced on their journey. On this page of Lewis's journal from February 24, 1806, the captain drew a sketch of a fish he had encountered on the expedition.

conditions were not easy for a group of high-spirited young men to take without complaint. After two and a half months, they were still in what is now the state of Missouri. The trip was supposed to be a high adventure, not one where the corps members got blisters pulling a tow rope and were continually swatting gnats and mosquitoes!

First Meeting with Indians

On July 29 the expedition met a Missouri Indian, one of the few survivors of that tribe, whose members had died in several smallpox epidemics. With him was a French trapper named La Liberte. The two men were sent to the village of the Oto Indians to arrange a meeting with the captains. Several days later, at a spot near the present-day city of Council Bluffs, Iowa, the first exchange of presents and speeches occurred. Lewis wrote,

> [A]fter brackfast we collected those Indians under an owning of our Main Sail, in presence of our Party paraded & Delivered a long Speech to them expressive of our journey the wishes of our Government, Some advice to them and Directions how they were to conduct themselves.[4]

Medals were given out, and the chiefs of the band also made speeches "promising two porsue the advice & Derections given them that they wer happy to find that they had fathers which might be depended on &c."[5] (Jefferson, as president of the United States, was referred to as the "Great Father.") A canister of

Captain Lewis & Clark holding a Council with the Indians.

This page from the journals of Lewis and Clark published in 1810 shows Captain Lewis making a speech to a group of local Indians.

gunpowder and a bottle of whiskey were among the presents. Demonstrations of the technical superiority of the Americans were an important part of the meetings with the tribes. An explosion from the loud and impressive air gun and a demonstration of how magnifying glasses could start a fire were always part of the show.

This general pattern was followed whenever the Corps of Discovery met with the chiefs of the Indian tribes. Some tribes were more willing to accept this assumption of leadership and be addressed as "children" than were others. What must the Indians have thought about these white men, ascending the river into *their* land, telling them that they must follow the advice and rules of some Great Father whom they had never seen? We do know that all the promises, on both sides, were not kept. If the Indians had known what was going to happen later to their land and their freedom, it is doubtful that the expedition would have been treated so kindly.

Disciplining the Corps

During the Oto visit, one of the expedition's privates disappeared. Several Indians found Private Moses Reed hiding in their village and brought him back to the campsite. He had attempted to desert and had to be dealt with severely. The Oto chiefs were shocked at the punishment.[6] Reed had to "run the gauntlet." That is, he had to run four times through a corridor of all the enlisted men who each lashed him with willow switches. The chiefs said they would never inflict such indignity on one of their own men. If someone did something terrible in their society, they would kill him rather than humiliate him. The problem of Reed's deserting a small group on such a long march and the possible effect on the discipline of all the men was explained to the Oto. All of this occurred on Lewis's thirtieth birthday, August 18, so the evening was spent dispelling the bad mood, and both the expedition's men and the Indians danced to Pierre Cruzatte's fiddle. Reed would be sent home when the expedition reached its winter camp.

Discipline problems had arisen before as the band was shaping into the cooperative unit it would become. Three men were disciplined severely, with lashes. Private Alexander Willard, on night guard duty July 11–12, fell asleep on his post. He was found by Sergeant John Ordway and reported to the captains. This offense was punishable by death. What might have happened if hostile Indians had come along while Willard was snoring? Since that might have meant the death of many of the men and the failure of the expedition, sleeping on guard duty was a very serious crime. Though the captains did not sentence Private Willard to death, they did give him one hundred lashes, to be administered each day, for four days. Though this may seem very harsh, the success of the expedition depended on rules being obeyed absolutely.

By the end of August, there was no need for more severe disciplinary action. The Corps of Discovery was falling into place, thanks to the wise leadership of Meriwether Lewis and William Clark.

Death of a Sergeant

A tragedy and a near tragedy awaited the men when they reached what is now Iowa. In mid-July many of the men became sick with flulike symptoms. Sergeant Charles Floyd was also ill, but as the other men recovered, his symptoms increased. What is now believed to have been appendicitis—which could not have been cured in those days even in a large city with good doctors—worsened rapidly. On August 20 the boats pulled over to a bluff, "on the starboard side." Sergeant Floyd whispered, "I am going away," and died.[7]

This young man, who had just turned twenty-two, was buried on "Floyd's Bluff," near present-day Sioux City, Iowa. Patrick Gass was elected to take Floyd's place as sergeant (becoming the first man to win an election west of the Mississippi), and the group moved on. Amazingly, Charles Floyd's would be the only death of an expedition member on the entire trip.

The near tragedy began when Private George Shannon, the youngest member of the expedition, got lost while out hunting. John Colter, also young but an expert woodsman, was sent out to look for Shannon, but could not locate him. After sixteen days, Shannon arrived at camp—thin, hungry, and bedraggled, but safe. Shannon reported that when he had run out of

This is a view of the monument erected in memory of Sergeant Charles Floyd, the only member of the Lewis and Clark expedition to die on the journey.

bullets, but not gunpowder, he killed one rabbit by putting a sharp stick in his gun and shooting it.[8] However, for the last two weeks he had lived on nothing but grapes and plums.

Entering the Great Plains

As the expedition progressed, the landscape began to change. There were very few trees. The land flattened and became the Great Plains. The members of the expedition were from places where forests were lush. The flat, rolling, treeless landscape amazed them. They encountered new varieties of animals such as the antelope, which they called a beardless goat at first. The mule deer got its name from its large ears, which made it unlike the eastern variety of deer. Endless herds of buffalo roamed, and new plants, fruits, and grass rolled on to the horizon.

A full day was spent flushing a prairie dog from its hole. These little animals, which the expedition members called barking squirrels, lived in a four-acre underground "apartment house." They were very hard to catch. One day, all but a few men who were left to watch the boats traveled up the riverbanks and across the grass with buckets of water. Finally, one very wet prairie dog emerged sputtering from its nest. This interesting little specimen would travel back to Monticello after the winter encampment, along with other birds, plants, and animals—still alive.

As the Corps of Discovery moved farther along the Great Plains, they began to see buffalo moving across the land.

Meeting the Yankton Sioux

While Shannon, who got lost hunting as the expedition was about to meet the Oto Indians, was groping his way across the plains, the expedition crossed paths with the first band of Sioux Indians. On August 30 the Yankton Sioux pitched their painted buffalo-skin tepees across the river from the Corps of Discovery. The captains raised a flagstaff with the Stars and Stripes. Many speeches were made and presents handed out, as well as the usual demonstrations of the superior American technology.

Lewis began his systematic collection of notes about the Indians' customs, dress, social organization, ceremonies, games, and anything else about them that he thought Jefferson would want to know. He also started working on the impressive Indian vocabulary lists that he wanted to bring back with him. All went well during this first extended visit with an influential Missouri River tribe. According to a legend of the Yankton Sioux, a baby boy was born to the Indians during the encampment, and Lewis wrapped him in a United States flag and declared him an American.[9]

The main thing that the captains wanted to convey to the Indians was that their Great Father was now Thomas Jefferson, the president of the United States. They promised to help and protect the Indians in return for peaceful passage, information about the tribes upriver, and an opportunity to trade furs in the future. They urged the Yankton Sioux to make peace with other tribes.

Dancing, singing, and friendly relations marked the two-day encampment. But the Yankton Sioux warned the captains that the tribes above them on the river might not be so friendly. Lewis and Clark were particularly concerned about the Teton, or Lakota, Sioux, who had controlled trade goods and intimidated traders going up the Missouri for years. The Teton Sioux had heard that the Corps of Discovery was coming, and they did not plan to give up their total control of the area without a fight.

One more near disaster was to occur before the meeting with the Teton Sioux. On September 20 the corps camped on a sandbar in the river. Some men slept on the boats and some on the ground. They were fast asleep when a sudden lurch of the keelboat and a loud shot from the guard woke up everyone to a terrifying spectacle. The riverbanks were caving in, and the sandbar they were sleeping on simply disappeared! The men and boats escaped just moments ahead of a rush of clay, sand, and water.

Problems with the Teton Sioux

Near present-day Pierre, South Dakota, on the morning of September 25, the expedition met the Teton Sioux. It was, indeed, a very different encounter from that with the Yankton Sioux.

The captains pulled out the full regalia, firing the air gun and attempting to hand out medals and presents, most of which were laughed at. Captain Clark and a crew of expedition members rowed the chiefs

Black Buffalo, the Partisan, and Buffalo Medicine out to the keelboat.

When Clark rowed them back to shore, the Indians demanded more presents *and* Clark's boat. Three Indians took hold of the tow rope. The Partisan pushed Clark. Clark took out his sword and said he "felt myself grow warm."[10] Lewis, in the keelboat, told the men to ready their guns. Thirty Indian warriors readied their bows and arrows. On the keelboat, the cannon was loaded. Black Buffalo and Captain Clark shouted at each other for a while, and then Black Buffalo directed the Indians to let go of the boat. A moment that could have changed history had passed, though danger still hung in the air. The other chiefs would not shake hands with Clark, but Black Buffalo asked to be able to spend the night on the keelboat and to have the women and children of his village come down to the riverbank to see the boats.

The next day the Indians, with an apparent change of heart, carried the captains in buffalo robes to their village. Again, many drums pounded, and dancing, singing, and general celebration occurred. Buffalo meat, ground potatoes, and dog—an Indian delicacy—were served. Still, the captains were wary, especially when they heard a rumor that the Indians meant to kill them all the next day!

After a second day in the village, accompanied by some general confusion and another attack from the Partisan, the boats set off. Black Buffalo had decided to travel upriver with the expedition to the Arikara village.

It is possible that the Indians who ran along the bank, threatening to stop the expedition, did not want to fill their chief full of arrows. The next day Buffalo Medicine also joined the group for a day. The Sioux were no different from other societies, where certain individuals conform or go against the group. Luckily for the expedition, there were two chiefs who thought better of pursuing warlike tendencies. Though the captains would have preferred these two peaceful chiefs to stay with the expedition longer than a few days, their presence helped ensure the safe passage up the river.

The Arikara Indians

The next tribe the expedition encountered was the Arikara. These Indians were alternately peaceful and warlike and were currently at war with the Mandan Indians. Lewis and Clark very much wanted to convince the Arikara chiefs that peace was a good idea. The Mandan were just up the river, and friendly relations with both tribes would help the expedition pass a safe and productive winter.

The usual speeches were made and presents given, and the visit was pleasant. York, a black man who came on the expedition as William Clark's servant, was a particular favorite, because the Arikara had never seen anyone so dark-skinned or so large before. He and the other men joined in dances and games with the Arikara braves. The result was that an Arikara chief agreed to go along with the expedition to the Mandan villages and tell the people there that the Arikara wanted peace.

It was October 13 when the expedition left the Arikara village and started up the Missouri once again. Winter was coming. In the distance, snow covered the mountains, and frost nipped the morning air.

The captains had wanted to find the headwaters, the origination point, of the Missouri before they camped for the winter. Though they had traveled 1,609 miles from St. Louis, they were only now arriving at the last known place on their maps. They hoped their reception at the Mandan villages would be a good one—but what if it were not?

The Mandan Indians and their neighbors, the Hidatsa, were prosperous farmers. In 1804 they lived in five villages located near the present-day city of Bismarck, North Dakota, with a population of around forty-five hundred. These tribes were experienced at trading with other Indians and Europeans. When the Corps of Discovery reached the villages in late October, the Mandan welcomed them and invited them to spend the winter in the area.

WINTER AT FORT MANDAN

Building a Camp for the Winter

The corps needed to find a spot to build a winter fort that was well supplied with wood, and close to where the hunters could kill game. After several searches, Captain Clark, scouting with four of the corpsmen, located a spot just opposite the lower Mandan village, seven miles below the mouth of the Knife River. The expedition members began building a fort on November 2 and moved into it in mid-November.

The weather was extremely cold that winter. On December 17, Clark noted that the temperature was 45°F below zero. Even the river was frozen. Prior to that date, the men had hunted for food to get them through the winter, made warm clothing from skins, and made tools and canoes for the trip ahead. For most of the rest of the winter they survived on a diet of dried meat and corn, as game became scarce and no hunter could stay outdoors very long.

On December 7, Lewis and fifteen corpsmen had joined the Mandan on a buffalo hunt. These hardy young Americans were extremely impressed when the Indians, riding bareback, not only outrode them, but killed more buffalo as well.

But it was time to settle down, write up notes, and prepare boxes of specimens to send back to President Thomas Jefferson. The keelboat, with notes, boxes, and ten men, including the deserter, Moses Reed, would go back to St. Louis when the ice broke in the spring.

Living with the Mandan

The Mandan were friendly and helpful. Often the men of the two different cultures would get together and exchange music and dances. Once again, York was very popular and he took full advantage of this. He made wild roars and faces, and the Indian children squealed and came back for more.

Christmas Day was celebrated without the Indians, who were told that this was a great and special feast day for the Americans. Sergeant Ordway wrote in his journal:

> We fired the Swivels at day break & each man fired one round. our officers Gave the party a drink of Taffee [a warm alcoholic drink], we had the Best to eat that could be had, & continued firing dancing & frolicking dureing the whole day. . . . We enjoyed a merry cristmas dureing the day & evening untill nine oClock—all in peace & quietness.[1]

So a long winter continued to pass as pleasantly as could be expected in such cold weather, with the excitement of crossing a continent ahead.

On January 5, 1805, the Indians held a buffalo medicine dance, designed to call to the spirits of the buffalo and lure them near camp. They invited the expedition members to join them. The ceremonies lasted for three days. When buffalo appeared a few days later, most of the expedition members joined the Indians in the hunt, once again marveling at the riding and hunting skills of the Mandan.

By early February, food was getting very scarce. One of the ways the corps obtained corn, to be ground into meal, was through barter of services. John Shields and the other blacksmiths forged blades, which the Indians needed, and traded them for corn. The Indians drove a hard bargain, emphasizing their need for tools before they would give the expedition members the corn they needed. Lewis said, ". . . I believe it would have been difficult to have devised any other method to have procured corn from the natives."[2]

Enter Sacagawea

Shortly after the fort was built, a French fur trader named Toussaint Charbonneau came into camp with three young Indian women, one of whom was his wife, Sacagawea. She was a Shoshone girl, about sixteen years old. As a young girl, she had been captured by the Hidatsa and sold to Charbonneau. The captains hired Charbonneau as an interpreter, because he spoke English, French, and Hidatsa, and told him to bring Sacagawea. There was one problem: Sacagawea was pregnant, due to give birth at any time. This was hardly a trip suited for a woman about to become a mother! Even though travel with an infant was normal among the Indians, the captains' decision to hire Charbonneau and let him take Sacagawea along was unusual. It is a sign of how important the captains felt their contact with the Shoshone would be. The captains thought it was crucial that they find and talk with the Shoshone when the time came that they would need to travel by horseback. And they believed that Sacagawea could be of great help as an interpreter.

On February 11, still in the coldest part of winter, Sacagawea showed signs that she was about to give birth. She had a very difficult labor that went on for many hours. A French trapper named René Jessaume told Lewis that a potion of the rattle of a snake crushed and given in water could ease pains and help in delivery.

Lewis had, in his store of specimens, one of these rattles. Whether or not this was actually helpful will never be known for certain, but ten minutes after Sacagawea took a drink of this concoction she "brought forth [delivered her baby]."[3] The newborn child, Jean-Baptiste Charbonneau, became the youngest member of the Corps of Discovery.

On March 12, however, the possibility of Toussaint Charbonneau and his family accompanying the expedition appeared to be over. Charbonneau had decided he did not like the deal he was being offered. He refused to stand guard like the other men; he wanted to only carry what he chose and to be able to leave the expedition at any time he wanted if he felt insulted. Charbonneau said he would go along, but only as interpreter. Lewis, not a man to fool around with, told him to "be off the engagement, which was only virbal."[4] The Charbonneaus moved out of Fort Mandan, taking with them the captains' hope of trading horses with the Shoshone. Luckily for the expedition, however, on March 17, Charbonneau sent word that he apologized. He wished to go anyway and would agree to the captains' terms.

During this long winter, the captains found out that a division of Spanish soldiers and Comanche Indians had been dispatched to find and stop their expedition. The Spanish government was worried that the expedition would enter Spanish territory, particularly Texas, and claim it for the United States.

Another bit of information, brought to the fort by Drouillard, was that the Teton Sioux intended to follow the expedition and destroy it when spring arrived. Fortunately, neither group of potential enemies managed to find them and stop the expedition from proceeding. The Arikara chief had also made peace, for the moment, with the Mandan chiefs, and that alliance could prove to be useful.

The Mandan and Hidatsa helped the captains plan for what lay ahead. Clark made a map based on the information given to him by the Hidatsa. They told Clark that the Great Falls of the Missouri was only two or three days ahead and would only require a half-day portage. This was good news, because a portage meant that the boats had to be carried overland for the distance covered by the falls. There was much heavy equipment in the boats and the ground was difficult to traverse. Lewis and Clark hoped the Indians were right. If so, they could make it to the Pacific Ocean, and back to St. Louis, before they had to camp again for the winter.

First Report to the President

On April 7, 1805, the keelboat and its passengers and cargo set off down the now ice-free river. In it was more information about the country west of the Mississippi River than had ever been collected. There was information about climate, soil conditions, vegetation, animals, and the native people and how they lived. There were 108 botanical specimens, 68 mineral specimens, a large variety of animals and animal parts, four magpies, the no-longer wet prairie dog, and a prairie grouse. (However, on the trip back east, one magpie killed the rest of the birds, so Jefferson received only that one magpie and the prairie dog alive.)

Lewis sent back a detailed report to Jefferson on everything they had seen and the information they had been given by the Indians. This report totaled almost forty-five thousand words. Also included was the invaluable map Clark made of the route they had traveled and what, through conversations with the Indians, they expected to find ahead.

On April 6, Lewis had written:

> Our vessels consisted of six small canoes, and two large perogues. This little fleet altho' not quite so rispectable as those of Columbus . . . were still viewed by us with as much pleasure as . . . deservedly famed adventurers ever beheld theirs; and I dare say with quite as much anxiety for their safety and preservation. we were now about to penetrate a country at least two thousand miles in width, on which the foot of civilized man had never trodden; the good or evil it had in store for us was for experiment yet to determine, and these little vessells contained every article by which we were to expect to subsist of defend ourselves.[5]

At 5:00 P.M. that day, a now totally disciplined group of men, one woman, and a baby set off into the unknown. Thirty-three people in six dugouts and two larger canoes continued into what is now Montana. No white person had ever gone farther on the river.

About 5 p.m. my attention was struck by one of the party runing at a distance towards us and making signs and hollowing as if in distress. . . . I immediately turned out with seven of the party in quest of this monster, we at length found his trale and persued him about a mile by the blood . . . . these bear being so hard to die reather intimedates us all; I must confess that I do not like the gentlemen and had reather fight 2 Indians than one bear. . . .[1]
—Captain Meriwether Lewis,
May 11, 1805

★5★

OF BEARS AND BUFFALO

The "monster" that Meriwether Lewis referred to in this passage from his journal was none other than the granddaddy of all bears, the grizzly. Despite Lewis's poor spelling, his description of this encounter is most clear. As the expedition traveled west into Montana, game became scarce. The meat, skin, and oil of a large bear could be very useful for food and clothing—but these animals were most unwilling to cooperate! There are many instances in the men's journals of their being chased into the river or run up a tree by a bullet-riddled grizzly. Lewis wrote, "There is no other chance

An American having struck a Bear but not killed him, escapes into a Tree.

This page from the journals published in 1810 shows a member of the Corps of Discovery who has escaped from a grizzly bear by climbing up a tree.

to conquer them by a single shot but by shooting them through the brains . . . the flece and skin were as much as two men could possibly carry."[2]

Problems of the Expedition

Finding game—without getting chased up trees while trying to shoot it—was a constant worry. The all-meat diet of the men was also not healthy, though few people knew that in 1805. Here, Sacagawea first proved herself to be a valuable member of the expedition. When game became scarce, she gathered prairie turnips and Jerusalem artichokes, root vegetables buried just beneath the surface of the soil. As she walked along the riverbank or rode in the canoes, her baby on her back, she was always watchful for possible sources of food beneath her feet.

The large canoes, or pirogues, had a crude sail. Headwinds, winds that came directly at the boat, were fierce along the river. One day a "sudon squawl of wind struck her [the boat] obliquely, and turned her considerably, the steersman allarmed, in stead of puting, her before the wind, lufted her up into it."[3] This is sailing language that means the man steering turned the boat directly into the sudden wind, which was so strong that it turned the canoe over "and would have turned her completely topsaturva" if the men had not rowed hard.[4] All the men were working hard to right the canoe—except for Charbonneau, who had been controlling the rudder. Charbonneau was wailing and did not calm down and take hold of the rudder again until Pierre Cruzatte, an expert sailor, threatened to shoot him.

Imagine the scene—boxes of medicine, supplies, and trade goods had been knocked overboard. Everyone was yelling and the wind was howling. Meanwhile, Sacagawea, who was onboard the unfortunate canoe, set about gathering up the articles that were washed overboard. In Lewis's words: "The Indian woman to whom I ascribe equal fortitude and resolution, with any person onboard at the time of the accedent, caught and preserved most of the light articles which were washed overboard."[5] Sacagawea was not only very brave and steady, but had the good sense to gather up the important things that otherwise could have been lost forever.

During this last week of May, the expedition traveled a section of the Missouri River that is still one of the truly isolated parts of the country. Designated a Wild and Scenic River by Congress in 1944, this 160-mile stretch runs from present-day Fort Peck Lake to Fort Benton, Montana. The eastern half is called the Missouri River Breaks, followed by the White Cliffs area. Here, the river zigzags so much that the expedition actually ended up traveling west, northwest, north, and then southwest.

While finding it difficult going, Lewis described the wild beauty of the White Cliffs as seeming almost to have been built by humans, like a city in ruins, rising some nearly three hundred feet straight up.[6] This stretch of the river can still be seen only by canoe, and several river outfitters now take travelers for three- or four-day camping trips down the river.

White Cliffs is also one of the driest parts of the United States. Lewis was amazed when the joints of some of his instruments came loose because all lubrication had evaporated. The dry air was drinking up all moisture.[7]

In addition to the beauty of the land and the amazement the expedition members felt at the dryness of the air, they were encountering new animal and plant species every day. It was here that the expedition first found the bighorn sheep.

Clark observed a beautiful clear stream and named it the Judith River for the girl at home whom he hoped to marry. (The fact that this woman, who later became his wife, was named Julia, not Judith, Hancock, is just part of Clark's very individual spelling.) This was just one of the many rivers, mountains, and bluffs named by the members of the expedition.

The Dilemma of the Forks

By now the men expected to see the Great Falls at any moment. On June 1 the river made a large bend, sending the expedition southwest. When the party camped for the night on the south shore, they saw, instead of the Great Falls, a large river flowing into the Missouri. The Mandan and Hidatsa had not mentioned any such river. They had told the captains about the Milk River, a large northern tributary of the Missouri, which they had passed a month ago. But what was this river? Which fork was the Missouri? What would they do now?

There were two possible choices—the "real" Missouri could be either the north fork or the south fork of the rivers that lay ahead. Though all of the men on the expedition believed that the true Missouri lay to the north, they still agreed to follow their captains in whichever direction they thought was correct. The expedition, after taking extensive exploratory trips up both forks, turned south.

In the process of exploring the countryside around the two rivers, there occurred one of the most dangerous events of the journey. Lewis, along with Private Richard Windsor and several other men, was exploring along the river bluffs above the north fork, which Lewis had named the Marias River. The day was rainy and the soil wet. Lewis slipped and nearly fell about ninety feet into the river. He reacted quickly and saved himself with "my espoontoon"—a spontoon, or a spike with a sharp point. Lewis wrote that he was barely able to stand when he heard Windsor cry, "god, Captain, what shall I do. . . ." Lewis wrote:

> on turning about I found it was Windsor who had sliped and fallen abut the center of this narrow pass and was lying prostrate on his belley, with his wright hand arm and leg over the precipice while he was holding on with the left arm and foot as well as he could which appeared to be with much difficulty.[8]

Windsor was about to plunge into the river! Lewis was alarmed because of Windsor's dangerous position over the precipice. He also saw that Windsor was so frightened that he might let go with the hand and arm that were clutching the muddy, slippery soil. Lewis, a great leader and someone who thought very quickly, realized he could not show Windsor that he was frightened for him. Lewis assured Windsor calmly that he was not in danger. In this way he helped Windsor clear his mind enough to follow Lewis's directions. Imagine taking a knife out of your belt with the hand that is dangling ninety feet above a roaring river and being calm enough to dig a hole in the bank with it! Windsor was able to do it because of his trust in Captain Lewis. He put his foot in the hole and then took off his moccasins and crawled to safety. And he did all this while holding his gun in the hand above the precipice and his knife in the hand that was hanging over the river!

If Private Windsor had not been used to following the orders of Captain Lewis, a leader he trusted, this episode could have turned out badly. The discipline exacted from the expedition members at the beginning of the journey had paid off by saving their lives.

Captain Lewis had named the river at the fork flowing from the north the Marias, after one of his favorite cousins from Virginia. Knowing that whatever they found, they would at some point come to the end of river travel, they left behind one of the large canoes, or pirogues. They also cached, or buried, items that they would not need until the return trip.

Searching for the Great Falls

When the expedition turned south, along what the captains believed was the true Missouri, much hung in the balance. Would they be right? If they were not, the expedition would surely fail. Captain Lewis and a small group of men went ahead of the boats, scouting for the Great Falls. On June 13, Lewis saw something that amazed him—cascading water, some eighty feet high and three hundred yards wide.[9] Here was the Great Falls of the Missouri. But it was not just one waterfall. In addition to the one huge waterfall, there were four others.

None of the falls was navigable by canoe. This was no half-day portage. The expedition would have to carry the boats and baggage around all five falls. Meanwhile, Captain Clark and the rest of the party had been traveling on the river. On June 14, Joe Field, who had been at the Great Falls with Captain Lewis, met the canoe party with news from Lewis about the discovery of the falls. The river, at this point, was very difficult to navigate. In Clark's words:

> the current excessively rapid and dificuelt to assend great numbers of dangerous places, and the fatique which we have to enconter is incretiatable the men in the water from morning untill night hauling the cord & boats walking on sharp rocks and round sliperery stones which alternately cut their feet and throw them down, notwith standing all this dificuelty they go with great chearfulness.[10]

On June 13, 1805, Meriwether Lewis reached the Great Falls of the Missouri River, shown here.

Sacagawea was also extremely ill with what historians believe was a urinary tract infection. By the time Clark and his party arrived at the encampment below the falls, her fever was high. Lewis was worried:

> I reached the camp found the indian woman extreemly ill and much reduced by her indisposition. this gave me some concern as well for the poor object herself, then with a young child in her arms, as from the consideration of her being our only dependence for a friendly negociation with the Snake Indians [the Shoshone] on whom we depend for horses to assist us in our portage from the Missouri to the columbia river.[11]

Fortunately for all concerned, Sacagawea recovered after drinking the water from a sulfur spring. Sulfur is helpful in killing bacteria, and although Lewis did not know that was the reason, folklore had spoken for centuries about sulfur's healing properties. Lewis once again used his rudimentary medical knowledge to save a life, something he did frequently for both expedition members and Indians during the trip.

Portaging the Falls

At this time, however, plans had to be made for the first portage around those intimidating falls. Clark found that the shortest route was about eighteen miles in length, on the south side of the river. Wagons had to be built to haul the boats and equipment. Two crude carts of cottonwood were constructed. Harnesses of buckskin were made and worn by the men who pulled

This is the map of the expedition's portage around the Great Falls drawn by William Clark.

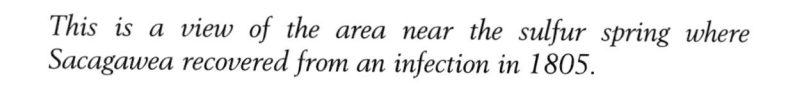

This is a view of the area near the sulfur spring where Sacagawea recovered from an infection in 1805.

the wagons. The pirogue was too large to carry, and it was left below the falls. More baggage was cached in this lower portage campsite. After days of complicated and intense preparation, the expedition was finally able to attempt the trip around the Great Falls. The portage, which was to last nearly three weeks and take four round trips, had begun.

The countryside in the portage area was filled with wildlife. This was good for hunting game to fill the stomachs of tired and hungry men. It also meant, however, that the danger of grizzly attacks or charging buffalo was constant, as well as the threat of snake bites. The mosquitoes were again "extreemly troublesome," but the worst was the soil itself.[12] Buffalo hooves had made the ground rutted and sharp, and prickly pear cactus was everywhere. These buckskinned men had to make new moccasins every two days, putting on double soles and repairing them each night. They were so tired they would stop for a rest and fall sound asleep right where they dropped. Violent storms and flash floods often made them dash for whatever cover they could find, just to keep from being hurled from the banks of the river into the falls and raging river below.

When the portage was finished, the expedition remained at the falls an extra week to complete construction on a large iron-frame boat, which Lewis had designed in 1803. The boat was collapsible, and the frame had been transported from St. Louis. Skins were to be sewn together over the frame, thus making up for the abandoned pirogues. Sometimes the best plans

This is a prickly pear cactus, which caused much trouble for the members of the Lewis and Clark expedition.

do not work out—and this one did not. The corpsmen could not find the right pine pitch or needles to sew the hides together and seal them. Much to Lewis's dismay, the iron boat had to be abandoned. Two more cottonwood dugouts had to be built to replace it, and more baggage cached. This extra delay, however, allowed the men to set in a large store of dried meat and fish for the trip ahead. They also made pemmican, a high-energy food the Indians had taught them about, which consisted of dried meat, ground fine and mixed with melted fat. Nevertheless, it was a frustrating delay. Would they meet the Shoshone in time to get horses and cross the mountains before winter?

Finally, on July 15 the expedition set out. Lewis and Clark and two of the corpsmen walked on shore. They wanted to lighten the loads of the canoes and to scout for signs of Indians. Horse tracks and willow shelters, appearing to be about ten days old, were found. Had they found the Shoshone at last?

It was good to leave camp and get back on the river. Lewis and Clark had seen signs of Indians when they were scouting along the riverbanks. They could see obvious Indian routes, recently traveled. Sap and the soft part of wood and bark were often used for food by the Indians, and it was encouraging to find pine trees with peeled-off bark.

HORSES AND HIGH MOUNTAINS AHEAD

Finding the Shoshone

Navigating the river was increasingly difficult. The men were using their tow lines and poles constantly. On July 19 the party reached a point in the river with "the most remarkable" cliffs Lewis had ever seen.[1] The cliffs were twelve hundred feet high, and it seemed as though the river had worn a channel through them for three full miles. Lewis called this passage the Gates of the Rocky Mountains. Though they saw Indian fires near this area, the Indians still kept themselves hidden. The good news was that Sacagawea was beginning to recognize the area. She told the captains that this was

Captain Lewis called this area the Gates of the Rocky Mountains, where the river created a channel through the mountain walls.

the river on which her relatives lived. The three forks, where she was captured by the Hidatsa when she was about ten years old, were very nearby, she assured them.[2]

Lewis and Clark took turns taking parties out across the land to try to make contact with the Shoshone. The boats were having difficulty getting over the rapids, and mosquitoes were again causing great distress. By the time the expedition reached the Three Forks of the Missouri on July 27, game was becoming scarce. Lewis, traveling by land, left a note for Clark near the Big Hole River. He told Clark not to travel the way Lewis's party was going, but to wait for him there. Unfortunately, a beaver apparently gnawed on the green willow on which Lewis left the note and carted it off. So receiving no notification otherwise, Clark's party began ascending the swift and dangerous river. Two boats filled with water and one turned over before Lewis caught up with the party and told them to return to the fork they had named the Jefferson. Twenty-one days had passed since the expedition left the Great Falls of the Missouri.

One bright morning, Sacagawea recognized a large outcropping of land, which her people called the Beaver's Head. She was absolutely sure that the summer camp of her people was just ahead.[3] They lived on a river beyond the mountains, now called the Lemhi River.

By now there had been four ranges of mountains since the expedition left the Great Falls camp. Lewis,

An outcropping now called Beaverhead Rock, which Sacagawea recognized as a landmark near the summer camp of the Shoshone Indians.

walking with George Drouillard and Privates McNeal and Shields across a level plain, saw an Indian riding on horseback toward them. This was the first Indian the expedition had encountered in fourteen hundred miles. Though two miles away, Lewis could see that the Indian was dressed differently from other Indians they had met. He must be a Shoshone! The passage in the journals in which Lewis describes the meeting is more suspenseful than any Western movie. Four men are marching across a plain, with the sole purpose of finding the Shoshone Indians. Without the horses the Shoshone could give them, the expedition would probably fail. Finally, directly in front of them was one of the very people they wanted to find. Lewis advanced at a regular pace. His own words tell what happened next:

> I was overjoyed at the sight of this stranger and had no doubt of obtaining a friendly introduction to his nation provided I could get near enough to him to convince him of our being whitemen. I therefore proceeded towards him at my usual pace. when I had arrived within about a mile he made a halt which I did also and unloosing my blanket from my pack, I made him the signal of friendship known to the Indians of the Rocky mountains and those of the Missouri, which is by holding the mantle or robe in your hands at two corners and then throwing it up in the air higher than the head bringing it to the earth as if in the act of spreading it, thus repeating three times. . . .[4]

Unfortunately, Drouillard, Shields, and McNeal were still advancing behind and to the side of Lewis.

They were too far away to hear Lewis shout, and he was afraid to make any signal to them that might make the Indian bolt. Finally Drouillard and McNeal halted, but Shields kept coming, gun in hand. Lewis held up trinkets and lifted his shirt so that the white skin above his deep tan would be seen by the Indian. Even so, the Indian wheeled and whipped his horse across the creek and into the willow brush, Lewis wrote,

> and with him vanished all my hopes of obtaining horses for the preasent. I now felt quite as much mortification and disappointment as I had pleasure and expectation at the first sight of this indian. I felt soarly chargrined at the conduct of the men, particularly Shields to whom I principally attributed this failure in obtaining an introduction to the natives.[5]

It would not have been pleasant to be Private Shields at that moment in history!

The men immediately followed the track of the Indian's horse. Though they saw many Indian signs, it was not until two days later that their luck would turn. Before that time they would actually come to the very beginning of the mighty Missouri water, here only a small creek, "the most distant fountain of the waters of the mighty Missouri."[6] Hugh McNeal would stand with one foot on each side of the tiny stream that issued from the earth.

Reaching the Continental Divide

These four men would also cross the Continental Divide, the imaginary line running through North

This is a view of the Continental Divide, the point at which east-flowing rivers are divided from west-flowing rivers.

America that divides east-flowing rivers from rivers that flow westward. Climbing up a ridge beyond the Missouri source water, Lewis thought he had perhaps found the Northwest Passage, that elusive route that so many explorers had sought and had hoped would run east-west across the northwest part of the vast territory. Perhaps, with one day's portage they would reach the Columbia River. Instead, he saw more and more mountains: "We proceeded on to the top of the dividing ridge from which I discovered immence ranges of high mountains still to the West of us with their tops partially covered with snow."[7] This ended decades of hope that a Northwest Passage would provide practical access to the Pacific Ocean. According to historian Stephen Ambrose, "With Lewis's last step to the top of the Divide went decades of theory about the nature of the Rocky Mountains, shattered by a single glance from a single man."[8]

As the small group started descending the western side of the Bitterroot Mountains, they saw two Indian women, a man, and some dogs. The Indians disappeared behind a hill. About half a mile farther, they surprised three more women. One ran away, but an old woman and a girl of about twelve stayed, terrified, bending their heads as if they were about to die. After being given beads and paint, they agreed to take Lewis's party to their village.

Meeting the Shoshone

After two miles, sixty mounted warriors galloped up. One of them was the Shoshone chief, Cameahwait, whose name meant "He Who Never Walks." It was a fitting name for the chief of a band of Indians who were rich only in horses. Lewis was able to convince them of his friendly intentions, and

> these men then advanced and embraced me very affectionately in their way, which is by putting their left arm over your wright shoulder clasping your back, while they aply their left ceek to yours and frequently vociforate the word ah-hi-e, ah-hi-e that is I am much pleased i am much rejoiced. both parties now advanced and we were all acarresed and besmeared with their grease and paint till I was heartily tired of the national hug.[9]

Lewis asked the Indians to come with him to meet Clark and the larger party and to bring horses to portage their belongings to the Shoshone village. Though this frightened some of the women, twenty-eight warriors and three women went back with Lewis. The Shoshone had been raided frequently by neighboring tribes, especially the Hidatsa and the Blackfeet, and had retreated to their mountain hideaway. Their lodges were made of sticks because a group of Blackfeet had raided their village in the spring and stolen their skin lodges. They were taking a big chance by leaving their mountain hideaway with these strangers. However, when they saw Sacagawea with her baby on her back, the Indians were convinced that this was not a war party.

Here, the most remarkable coincidence of the trip occurred. When the captains were sitting with Cameahwait, beginning to barter for horses, Sacagawea was called to interpret. Suddenly, she jumped up and ran to Cameahwait, throwing her blanket around his shoulders and sobbing. Cameahwait, the chief of the Lemhi Shoshone, was Sacagawea's brother! It took a long time for the translating to start, because Sacagawea kept breaking into tears. But at last it began. Trade goods were put out, and the translation went from Cameahwait who spoke Shoshone, to Sacagawea who spoke Hidatsa, to Charbonneau who spoke French better than he spoke English, to expedition member Francis Labiche, who translated into English for the captains. Despite this long proceeding, by the end of the day all the horses the Shoshone could spare were bartered.

August 18 was Lewis's thirty-first birthday. He wrote in his journal in a reflective way. Instead of praising himself for the success of the journey thus far, he scolded himself for being "indolent," or lazy, and vowed to live from then on to help all mankind.[10] This was just one example of Lewis's very serious nature. Though he was a brilliant leader, he was often very hard on himself. However, Lewis's attitude did not prevent him from proceeding on all through the journey and from thinking quickly in a crisis. Today, we can hardly imagine the kind of bravery Lewis, Clark, and most of the expedition members, including Sacagawea, exhibited daily.

While with the Shoshone, Lewis wrote in his journal about this impoverished but friendly tribe. He talked about their family life and marriage customs in great detail. Lewis mentioned that Sacagawea had been pledged in marriage, as a little girl, to a man much older than she was. The Hidatsa raid during which she was captured took place before she was thirteen, which was about the age that Shoshone girls were married. The man to whom she had been pledged was still living with the Shoshone, but he had two other wives. This Indian man said that because Sacagawea had a child by Charbonneau, he would no longer claim her as a wife. We can only wonder what would have happened if he had tried to claim Sacagawea. What would Charbonneau have done? Would this have caused trouble for the expedition?

Captain Clark had been exploring a river called the Salmon to see if it was navigable. He discovered that it was not, with the help of a Shoshone man the members of the expedition called Old Toby. This man gave them advice about the mountains ahead, and the captains decided to hire him to guide them across.

Setting Off Across the Mountains

At last, on August 25, 1805, the expedition was ready to begin the difficult passage through the Bitterroot Mountains, on an Indian trail that the Nez Percé (Pierced Nose) Indians used to reach the Missouri. The Shoshone told them that in ten days they would reach the Nez Percé village, and a river—the Clearwater, which fed into the Snake River—that was navigable. The corps members sunk their canoes in a nearby pond so they could retrieve them on the return trip, and cached more supplies. Sacagawea must have wept bitter tears at leaving her childhood home after she had finally returned. The journals, however, so full of reports of dangerous events and wondrous sights, do not tell us of her feelings as the expedition set off on its way once again.

OCEAN IN VIEW

With Old Toby as their guide, the expedition set out across the Bitterroot Mountains. They traveled along steep mountain walls. Many horses slipped, and the expedition's last thermometer was broken when the pack holding it fell down the steep mountainside. Snow, then rain and sleet, began to fall. Then Old Toby got lost, wasting four days.

Crossing the Bitterroots

On September 4 the expedition descended into a village of Salish, or Flathead, Indians at a spot called Ross's Hole. They were able to buy thirteen more horses, but the negotiations, though very friendly, took a whole day. Sergeant Ordway said that "these natives have the Stranges language of any we have ever yet seen. they appear to us as though they had an impedement in their Speech or brogue on their tongue. we think perhaps that they are the welch Indians. . . ."[1] Ordway referred to a myth that had long held sway in American history. According to legend, a group of Welshmen came to the New World in the twelfth

This mural, painted by artist C. M. Russell, depicts the Lewis and Clark expedition meeting the Salish, or Flathead, Indians at Ross's Hole.

century, and settled in the West, where their descendants lived on. Explorers frequently tried to find these Indians, some even reporting that they had found this group. But there is no proof that the Welsh Indians ever existed. Lewis, however, wrote quickly during the visit, hoping to record the Flathead names for everything and perhaps prove the theory at last. (As far as we know now, there was no truth to this myth.)

Soon, however, the Corps of Discovery had to leave these friendly, intriguing Flathead Indians and move on. One member of the tribe agreed to come with the expedition and introduce its members to his people on the other side of the mountains. They traveled down a valley, resting for a day at a camp they called Traveler's Rest. The expedition then turned west onto the Nez Percé trail.

When the expedition reached Lolo Pass, the most challenging part of their very difficult journey began. There was no game. They had to eat horses, candles, and the untasty portable soup, a concoction Lewis had made in great quantity in Philadelphia. They named one campsite Hungry Creek, because they had nothing to eat that night. Their horses slipped on the steep trail, one falling nearly one hundred yards down the mountain. Because of the poor diet, the men became weak with stomachaches, and they developed sores all over their bodies from hard riding. Snow was ahead on the mountains, and there were mountains on every side.

A view of the Lolo Pass, where the most challenging part of the expedition's journey began.

Meeting the Nez Percé

The snow was very heavy. With a small group of men, Captain Clark forged ahead of the weakened group and found a friendly Nez Percé village. He sent news back to the main body of the expedition, who struggled forward to meet him. It was a bedraggled and nearly starved group of men who arrived at the Nez Percé village after 165 torturous miles and eleven miserable days. Here, on the border of present-day Idaho and Washington, the Nez Percé hardly knew what to make of these weak and ill white men. Though the Corps of Discovery was not aware of it at the time, the consensus among the tribe was that the expedition members should be killed, making the tribe rich in trade goods, guns, and horses. However, a woman named Watkuweis, which means "Returned from a Far Country," interceded for them. She had been captured by a hostile tribe and sold to white people, who had treated her well. She sent word to the chief, Twisted Hair, that the kindness shown to her should be returned.[2]

The Nez Percé were very helpful to the Corps of Discovery. In more than two weeks' stay, while the men recuperated, the Indians drew maps of the country ahead for the expedition. The Indians showed the men how to burn out the inside of a ponderosa pine tree to save labor when making dugouts. When the starving men first arrived, however, they ate heartily of camas root and salmon with bread. Unaccustomed to this kind of diet, they became even more ill, several nearly dying of intestinal problems. They recovered,

The friendly Nez Percé Indians taught the members of the Corps of Discovery how to burn tree trunks to build dugout canoes, like this one.

however, and on October 7 launched five new dugout canoes on the Clearwater River. Their horses, branded so they would be recognized, were left in the care of the Nez Percé until the return trip.

Since they had now crossed the Continental Divide, the current of the river was finally going in the right direction. They were now no longer in the United States, but in the Oregon Country, claimed by both Great Britain and the United States. The swift current hurtled them down the Clearwater and Snake rivers. The Indians remained friendly, and at one village the Indians' nervousness changed to pleasure when they saw Sacagawea and her baby. This could not be a war party if a woman accompanied it. Once again, Sacagawea was helpful to the expedition, this time protecting them just by her presence.

Reaching the Columbia

On October 16, they reached the Columbia River. The landscape was changing daily; game and firewood became scarce as they passed through semidesert. Walla Walla and Yakima Indians watched them pass. Salmon were seen jumping in the clear river water. But the men did not want fish—they were used to meat. Game was rare, and dog meat was the order of the day for everyone except Captain Clark, who could never get used to it.[3]

The expedition passed Mount Hood, the highest point of the Cascade Mountains. They passed through rapids, portaging some of them but taking chances on running others. They were impatient to reach their goal—the Pacific Ocean—and were excited by the new speed of travel. At the end of October they rowed into the great gorge of the Columbia River. Dense forests rose on both sides of the river. Waterfalls were everywhere, and the climate had changed so that the atmosphere was almost a rain forest.

The Indians they met were also different. The Chinook Indians flattened the heads of their infants by compressing their heads between boards. They looked strange, indeed, to the expedition members. These Indians lived in houses made of wooden planks and wore clothes made of cedar bark. The area was just as populated as the thirteen original colonies, whose population in 1801 had reached almost 6 million. Unfortunately, these Indians were not of the helpful, friendly disposition of the Mandan, Shoshone, and Nez Percé. They had been visited for many years by Europeans arriving by sea, and they demanded high prices for food and services. They also continually stole from the expedition's camps, whenever they could get away with it.

On the morning of November 7, 1805, the expedition started out in a dense fog. When the fog lifted, Captain Clark shouted, "Ocian in view. O the Joy!"[4] The entire Corps of Discovery must have felt thrilled at this sight, believing that they had finally reached their destination, the Pacific Ocean.

Though Captain Clark recorded his excitement in his journal, it turned out that this first view was not really the ocean, but a large bay a few miles from the Pacific. The party finally reached the Pacific Ocean on November 15, 1805. Bad weather marooned the expedition for three weeks at a place they called Cape Disappointment. When they were able to look for a perma-

WAITING OUT ANOTHER WINTER

nent winter campsite, the Chinook and Clatsop Indians advised them to go to the south shore of the Columbia River, a few miles from the ocean. They needed to be near the ocean in case a ship came with supplies and maybe even a ride home.

Setting Up Camp for the Winter

The captains did an unusual thing. They took a vote of the *entire* company about the location of the winter fort. This included York (Captain Clark's slave) and Sacagawea. This was decades before the Emancipation Proclamation and before women were given the right

AT A DISTANCE OF TWENTY MILES FROM OUR CAMP WE HALTED AT A VILLAGE. . . . WE HAD NOT GONE FAR FROM THIS VILLAGE WHEN THE FOG CLEARED OFF, AND WE ENJOYED THE DELIGHTFUL PROSPECT OF THE OCEAN; THAT OCEAN, THE OBJECT OF ALL OUR LABOURS, THE REWARD OF ALL OUR ANXIETIES. THIS CHEERING VIEW EXHILIRATED THE SPIRITS OF ALL THE PARTY, WHO WERE STILL MORE DELIGHTED ON HEARING THE DISTANT ROAR OF THE BREAKERS. WE WENT ON WITH GREAT CHEERFULNESS UNDER THE HIGH MOUNTAINOUS COUNTRY WHICH CONTINUED ALONG THE RIGHT BANK; THE SHORE WAS HOWEVER SO BOLD AND ROCKY, THAT WE COULD NOT, UNTIL AFTER GOING FOURTEEN MILES FROM THE LAST VILLAGE, FIND ANY SPOT FIT FOR AN ENCAMPMENT. AT THAT DISTANCE, HAVING MADE DURING THE DAY THIRTY-FOUR MILES, WE SPREAD OUR MATS ON THE GROUND, AND PASSED THE NIGHT IN THE RAIN.[1]

This excerpt from the journals of Lewis and Clark, dated November 7, 1805, expresses the expedition's excitement at finally reaching their destination—the Pacific Ocean.

to vote. It was just another instance of Lewis and Clark's fairness, and a reminder of how much like a family these thirty-three people had become.

They decided to stay on the south shore, in a cove near present-day Astoria, Oregon. By December 25, 1805, they had built and moved into Fort Clatsop, named after the nearby Clatsop Indians. The weather was rainy, cold, and unpleasant, but the men were in good health. New Year's Day, 1806, was toasted with water, because the liquor supply was long since gone, and the "feast" consisted of boiled elk and roots.[2] Still, the men's spirits were high because all knew that the homeward journey was just a winter away.

Though they survived mostly on poor elk meat and water, they passed the winter productively. One of the major tasks was to make salt, which they did by boiling ocean water. The kettles were kept boiling day and night. Moccasins had to be made for the home journey, as well as clothes and candles. Though the men had little fun, a bit of excitement came when a giant beached whale was spotted a few miles from camp in early January. The whale blubber could be rendered into fat and added to their poor diet, so the whale was an exciting discovery. This is the only instance when Sacagawea was said to have spoken up. Lewis wrote:

> The indian woman was very importunate to be permitted to go, and was therefore indulged; she observed that she had traveled a long way with us to see the great waters, and that now that monstrous fish was also to be seen, she thought it very hard she could not be permitted to see either.[3]

Sacagawea was allowed to go along to see the great whale.

The Clatsop and Chinook Indians were often inside the expedition's fort, but incidents of theft made their visits unpleasant. Still, maintaining friendly relations was important in case food ran out completely or if Indians spotted a sailing vessel and could inform the captains of its arrival.

Captain Clark worked on a map, revising the one he had made at Fort Mandan to add what they now knew existed. One of the most remarkable accomplishments of the whole expedition was that Clark was so accurate in calculating the miles they had gone. He correctly said they had traveled 4,162 miles. Clark's map was based on celestial observations, calculating latitude and longitude.

Lewis worked on his detailed descriptions of plant and animal species. In all, the expedition had encountered and described 122 animal species and 178 plant species never before cataloged by science.

Leaving Fort Clatsop

On March 23, the Corps of Discovery gave Fort Clatsop away as a gift to the Clatsop Indians and started for home. The remaining trade items could be held in just two bandannas, which was upsetting. However, they still had lead, gunpowder, and rifles. They also never ran out of paper and ink for those all-important journals.

Once again they were rowing against the current and impatience ran high. The Indians along the way were bothersome to them, and on April 11, Lewis's dog, Seaman, was stolen. Three soldiers followed the three Indians who had taken Seaman. When they realized they were being pursued, the Indians finally let the dog go.

On April 27 the expedition camped with the Walla Walla, relatives of the Nez Percé. The chief, Yellept, told Lewis of a shorter route east to the Lolo Trail. Talking with the Walla Walla was easier when it was discovered that a Shoshone woman lived in their village. She translated into Shoshone for Sacagawea, and then the usual complex interpretation route continued. Lewis was much appreciated for his medicinal skills here, especially when he helped relieve several people with very sore eyes. (This was thought to be the result of sun glare on the water as the Indians waited to spear salmon.) Lewis reported: "Several applyed to me today for medical aide, one a broken arm another inward fevers and several with pains across their loins, and sore eyes. I administered as well as I could to all."[4]

Chief Yellept gave Clark a beautiful white horse. In return, Clark gave Yellept his sword and a hundred rounds of ammunition. The night before the corps left the Walla Walla village, about a hundred Yakima Indians joined festivities that included Pierre Cruzatte, again with his trusty fiddle, square dances and reels, and a hop-and-chant dance with the huge crowd of Indians.

The weather and the traveling were again terrible and the game scarce. By the time the expedition reached the Nez Percé village on May 4, hunger was the main problem. They were very pleased to be back with the Nez Percé. Once again, both Lewis and Clark set up a makeshift hospital and cured many Indian ailments. Weather conditions forced the corps to remain with the Nez Percé into June. While there, the men of the corps and the young Indian braves played games and competitive sports and waited out the deep snow in the Bitterroots.

Beginning the Journey Home

Impatient to be on their way home, the expedition started out on June 15 in snow that was still at least six feet deep. The Lolo Pass was so covered with snow they could not find it. They had to turn back. This was the first time in the entire journey the Corps of Discovery had retreated. It would also be the last. Hiring three Indian guides who found the trail easily, they proceeded on to Traveler's Rest. This 156-mile trip took six days instead of the eleven it had taken them on the outward journey. Once again the expedition owed its forward motion, if not its very survival, to native peoples.

A risky decision had
been made at Fort
Clatsop. The expedition
would separate into two
groups on the return
journey to do further
exploration. Lewis, with
five Nez Percé guides,
nine men, and seventeen
horses, would explore the
northern-bound Marias
River. Clark would head
toward Three Forks and
explore the Yellowstone

THE RETURN TRIP

River, hoping to make contact with new Indian tribes.
With him would be fourteen men, Sacagawea, and
little Pomp, Captain Clark's nickname for Jean-
Baptiste Charbonneau.

Conflict with the Blackfeet

Lewis's trip was eventful and was nearly fatal for him.
On July 26, Lewis's party saw eight warriors in the distance. They were now deep in Blackfeet territory.
These fierce Indians already knew that their fur-trading
power was going to be threatened by the white men,
and they had no reason to be friendly. However,
medals were given out by Lewis and a peace pipe
smoked. The two groups camped together overnight.
In the morning Lewis awoke to shouting and saw

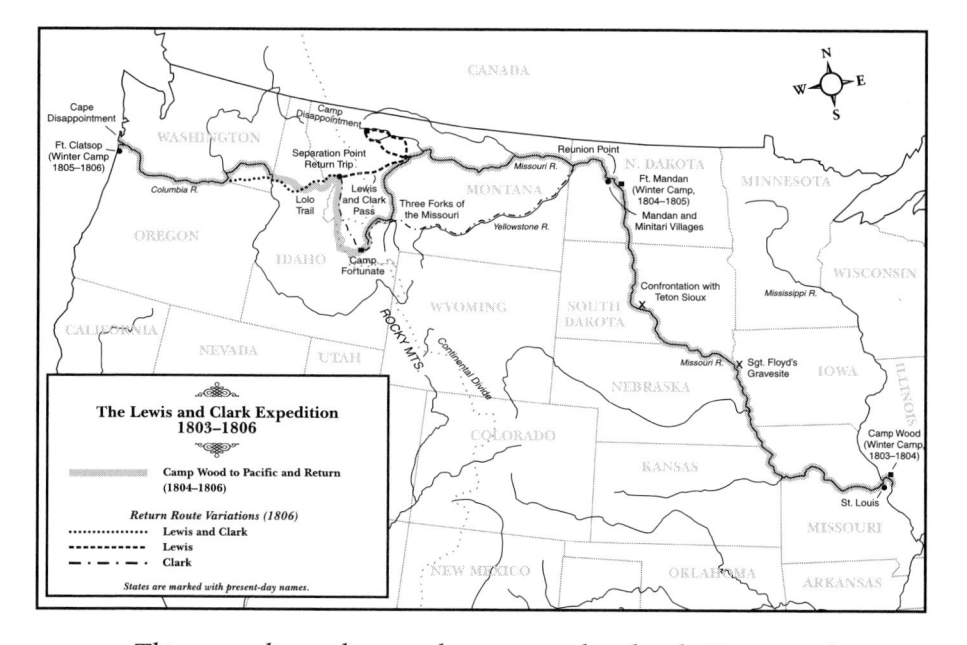

This map shows the complete route taken by the Lewis and Clark expedition to the Pacific Ocean and back to Missouri, including their two separate return routes in the area of Three Forks.

George Drouillard struggling with an Indian to get his rifle back. Joe and Reubin Field were chasing an Indian who held Joe Field's rifle. Reubin stabbed the Indian in the stomach.

Meanwhile, Lewis chased an Indian who had run off with his gun. The Indian shot at Lewis, who felt the bullet ruffle his hair. After grabbing another rifle, Lewis returned fire and killed the Blackfoot.

The Indians ran off, but Lewis and the other men knew they had to get out of that part of the country, fast! Leaving a medal around the Indian who was stabbed as a warning to other hostile Indians, they mounted their horses and rode hard. As Lewis recorded in the journals,

> Having no doubt that they [the Indians] would pursue us with a large party and as there was a band near the broken mountains or probably between them and the mouth of that river we might expect them to receive inteligence from us and arrive at that place nearly as soon as we could, no time was therefore to be lost and we pushed our horses as hard as they would bear.[1]

Riding night and day, they traveled 120 miles to their canoes. Then, they raced down Marias River to meet Clark.

Pompey's Pillar

While Lewis was in trouble in Blackfeet territory, Clark was inscribing his name and the date on a rock outcropping on the shore of the Yellowstone River, twenty-eight miles east of present-day Billings,

William Clark carved his name on this outcropping known as Pompey's Pillar on July 25, 1806.

Montana. On Pompey's Tower (now called Pompey's Pillar), William Clark wrote his name and the date—July 25, 1806. Though there have been rumors that other signatures were left along the trail, Clark's at Pompey's Pillar is the only signature that remains today on any of the trail landmarks.

Sacagawea pointed out many geographical points to Clark on this exploratory trip. When Clark's party of ten was exploring on foot, Sacagawea led them through Big Hole Pass, a gap in the mountains near present-day Jackson, Wyoming. This shortcut made the road back to their canoes easy. Speaking of yet another pass that saved time and effort, Clark recorded in his journal, "The Indian woman who has been of great Service to me as a pilot through this Country recommends a gap in the mountain more South which I shall cross."[2]

Lewis Is Accidentally Shot

Unlike Clark's experience, Lewis's homeward journey continued to be less than perfect. On August 7 he was out hunting with Pierre Cruzatte, who was blind in one eye and nearsighted in the other. Cruzatte mistook Lewis for an elk and shot him in the buttock. This pretty much immobilized Lewis, who had to lie on his stomach and be nursed by Clark, after the two parties reunited, for most of the rest of the journey.

The current was once more at their backs as the Corps of Discovery roared down the Missouri River. They pushed on to the Mandan villages where John

Colter, with the captains' permission, decided to go back up the Missouri to trap fur. He had been a very valuable hunter and guide on the expedition.

Return to the Mandan Villages

The Mandan were glad to see the members of the expedition but had bad news to report about wars between tribes. The visit of the Arikara chief, despite his good intentions, had not resulted in lasting peace. However, Big White, a Mandan chief, was willing to travel back to Washington, D.C., with Lewis and Clark to meet Thomas Jefferson.

Charbonneau, Sacagawea, and their son remained at the Mandan villages. For his services, Charbonneau was paid $500.33 1/3—and given his horse and tepee to keep. According to the custom of the time, Sacagawea, being a wife, was not paid anything personally, despite her great service to the expedition. Captain Clark, however, offered to take Pomp and raise him as his own son, when he was old enough to leave his mother. Clark later welcomed Pomp as a member of his household.

The Corps of Discovery had meetings with the Arikara and the Yankton Sioux and avoided the Teton Sioux on the way downriver. Soon they saw other boats traveling upriver and cows instead of buffalo became the backdrop along the banks.

Home at Last

At noon on September 23, the Corps of Discovery reached St. Louis, where five thousand people lined the banks to welcome the explorers home. Their fellow Americans cheered for these buckskinned, bearded men whom the entire country, and even President Jefferson, had given up for dead.

The last entry in the expedition's journal is brief. Captain William Clark stated, "a fine morning we commenced wrighting &c."[3]

Everywhere Lewis and Clark went in the weeks after their return, there were parties. They were treated to one celebration after another. The captains were rewarded with jobs and titles. Lewis was made governor of the territory of Upper Louisiana. Clark was appointed brigadier general of militia and superintendent of Indian affairs for the Louisiana Territory.

AFTERMATH AND THE TRAIL TODAY

Clark After the Expedition

William Clark went on to have a distinguished career. In all his work he was an advocate for Indian tribes. He married his sweetheart, Julia Hancock, and had several children. He married a second time after Julia died, and had two more children. Captain Clark also made good on his offer to raise Charbonneau and Sacagawea's son, Jean-Baptiste. He not only raised little Pomp, but also took in Sacagawea's second child, a girl named Lizette, who was born shortly before Sacagawea died at around age twenty-five, of what historians believe was the same kind of urinary tract infection she had successfully recovered from at the sulfur spring. Though much speculation has gone on over the years about the length of Sacagawea's life, reliable historians now believe there is no reason to doubt that she died young.[1] William Clark enjoyed a much longer life. He lived until age sixty-nine.

Lewis's Triumph and Tragedy

Meriwether Lewis, on the other hand, had a great deal of difficulty adjusting to the life of a politician. He was better suited to the continuous action and everyday discipline of the expedition. He had caught malaria at some point on the journey, a disease carried by mosquitoes. Malaria flares up again and again, causing high fevers and chills. Lewis was often sick and became very depressed.

The journals needed to be edited and published, and Lewis just could not seem to get around to it. He courted several women but never got engaged. When William Clark married, Lewis lived for a short time in the Clarks' home. Lewis seemed to need the support and friendship of his solid co-captain as much after the expedition as during it.

William Clark was very worried about his friend as Lewis set out on a road called the Natchez Trace in October 1809. By this time Lewis had many political and financial problems, and he was heading for Washington, D.C., to clear his name. In a boardinghouse along the way called Grinder's Inn, Meriwether

Lewis died. Some believe he may have been murdered, or his depression may have gotten the better of him and he may have died by his own hand. What really happened will never be known for sure, though historians generally believe it was suicide. Whatever the actual cause, Lewis's death was a great loss to the emerging United States of America.[2]

Results of the Expedition

The expedition had not found the Northwest Passage, because it did not exist. However, they had found what was then the most direct route across the new territory of the Louisiana Purchase to the West Coast. The scientific knowledge they brought back was tremendous, and the careful observation and systematic recording of data became a model for all future expeditions. In addition to the information on plant and animal species, Lewis compiled nine Indian vocabularies and provided detailed descriptions of various Indian tribes. Clark completed a map that was the best ever made, to that date, of the North American continent. This topographical information, coupled with the information on the tribes and the availability of fur-bearing animals to be hunted and trapped in the competitive fur trade, led to the development of the western United States. The most valuable result of the Lewis and Clark expedition was the extensive journals. These journals not only immortalized the information, but also the individuals who undertook and successfully completed this remarkable adventure.

The journals of Lewis and Clark were perhaps the most significant accomplishment of the expedition. With drawings and descriptions, as shown here, they provided Americans with important details about the territory of the Louisiana Purchase.

The Corps of Discovery was out there for 863 days, approximately two years and four months. In the days before the telegraph, telephone, radio, television, and computers, they had no way to communicate where they were and how they were doing. The Corps of Discovery had absolutely no communication with the rest of the world, except for the Indian tribes they met, from April 1805 until August 1806. Despite their almost complete isolation, they were not only able to survive, but to make many important scientific and geographical discoveries.

The Lewis and Clark Trail Today

Today, we can fly over the tremendous Bitterroot Range of the Rocky Mountains, which nearly took the lives of the members of the expedition. Outfitters now run hikes up the Lolo Pass and down the rapids of the Columbia Gorge. The National Park Service publishes maps of the trail and new trail markers are being put up every day. An organization called the Lewis and Clark Trail Heritage Foundation meets yearly in a town on the trail and visits Lewis and Clark sites. The foundation also publishes a magazine called *We Proceeded On*, a phrase used many times in the journals.

Though much of the trail has been obscured over time by the homes, businesses, and roads of modern America, a great deal of the rugged scenery in Montana, Idaho, and Washington State remains the same or similar to the beauty that the Corps of Discovery saw every day of that remarkable journey.

There are several archaeological surveys of sites along the Lewis and Clark trail now being undertaken. One is at Fort Clatsop and another at Fort Mandan. The "dig," as archaeologists call the sites they survey, at the lower portage camp, has been in operation each summer since 1987. The portage camp, where expedition members prepared wooden dugout canoes for the eighteen-mile trek along the riverbank, was the longest stopover with the exception of the winter camps. Surely, the members of the expedition left evidence there! Historical archaeologists Ken Karsmizki and Annalies Corbin direct a crew of archaeology interns and students who patiently dig and scrape the fine silt beneath the grass, hoping to unearth artifacts. Sometimes the finds are very small, such as a wooden tent stake of the sort used by soldiers in 1804, or bones that might have been from an expedition buffalo hunt. There were many campfires to keep warm and to cook their meat. Along the trail there were around six hundred campsites, but none has ever been absolutely confirmed by solid evidence.

Lessons of Lewis and Clark

We still have lessons to learn from Lewis and Clark. Some of those lessons are about nature and conservation. According to Dr. Daniel Botkin, some of the damage civilization has done to the environment can be corrected if we understand two lessons taught by the expedition.[3] One is that nature does not stand still; change is a natural, inevitable quality in nature. The

Today, there are several archaeological digs being undertaken along the trail followed by Lewis and Clark. This rain cover is protecting the site of one of these digs from bad weather.

other lesson is that what we appreciate in nature has often already been changed by humans. We need to understand how the environment has been changed before we can attempt to do things like reintroduce animal and plant species to the wilderness.

The lessons of survival, of kindness, of bravery, and of the necessity of self-discipline shine forth throughout the journals of Lewis and Clark. The value of friendship, the help of the American Indian tribes, without whom the Corps of Discovery could not have survived, are all chronicled in the amazing record kept by the members of the Corps of Discovery. The Lewis and Clark expedition is truly an American adventure story, and America at its best.

★ TIMELINE ★

1803—*July 4*: Newspaper reports that the Louisiana Territory has been sold to the United States by Napoleon.

July 5: Lewis leaves for Pittsburgh to make final arrangements for the journey.

October 26: Keelboat and pirogues leave Clarksville, with nine enlisted men and York.

December 9: Decision made to camp for the winter at Wood River, Illinois.

1804—*May 14*: The expedition gets under way, in a keelboat and two pirogues.

August 2: First contact with Indians.

August 20: Sergeant Charles Floyd dies, probably of appendicitis, near present-day Sioux City, Iowa.

September 23: During an encounter with the Teton Sioux, gunfire is barely avoided.

October 24: First meeting with the Mandan, including Chief Big White, who will travel with the expedition to St. Louis on the return trip.

November 3: Work on Fort Mandan, just opposite the lower Mandan village and seven miles below the mouth of the Knife River, is begun.

November 4: Toussaint Charbonneau visits Fort Mandan, offering the expedition his services as an interpreter and those of his wife, Sacagawea.

1805—*February 11*: Sacagawea gives birth to her son Jean-Baptiste Charbonneau, later called Pompey, or little Pomp, by Clark.

April 7: The keelboat heads back to St. Louis; The two pirogues and lighter canoes head upstream on the Missouri River; The expedition is now venturing into territory where no white men have gone before.

April 29: Expedition members shoot their first grizzly bear.

June 3: Two rivers, a north and south fork cause confusion about which is the true Missouri; The captains decide to follow the south fork; Windsor and Lewis nearly fall into the Missouri from a high embankment.

June 13: Lewis discovers the Great Falls of the Missouri.

June 22: The portage around the Great Falls begins.

July 27: Lewis finds Three Forks area of the Missouri River.

August 9: Lewis spots the first Shoshone Indian.

August 12: The Bitterroot Range of the Rocky Mountains is spotted.

August 13: Lewis and his exploratory party have their first meeting with the Shoshone.

August 17: Sacagawea discovers that the chief of the Shoshone band, Cameahwait, is her brother; The expedition trades for horses.

September 1: The expedition sets out to cross the Bitterroots, due north toward the Continental Divide.

September 21: Clark, who had gone ahead, sends news about a friendly Nez Percé village.

October 16: The expedition reaches the junction with the Columbia River.

November 7: The Pacific Ocean is in view.

December 6: The expedition members begin to build on the site to be called Fort Clatsop.

1806—*January 1*: The New Year is celebrated at Fort Clatsop.

March 23: The expedition leaves Fort Clatsop.

April 27: The expedition camps with the Walla Walla, relatives of the Nez Percé; Chief Yellept tells Lewis about a shorter route east to the Lolo Trail.

June 15: The party sets out, without Indian guides, and travels twenty-two miles.

June 16: Snow forces the expedition to retreat for the first and last time of the entire journey.

July 3: In order to explore the Marias River, the expedition is split into two groups; Lewis heads north while Clark heads toward the Three Forks.

July 7: Clark and a party of ten, including Sacagawea, cross Big Hole Pass.

July 22: Lewis, traveling up the Marias River, reaches the expedition's northernmost point.

July 26: Lewis and his party encounter Piegan Blackfeet.

August 11: Lewis is shot in the buttock, presumably by Pierre Cruzatte.

August 14: The expedition returns to the Mandan villages.

August 17: Charbonneau and his wife and son stay at the Mandan villages; Private John Colter is given permission to leave the expedition to trap fur.

September 22–23: The expedition passes its first winter camp at Wood River, and arrives in St. Louis, where enthusiastic crowds line the riverbank to greet its members.

People of the Expedition

Co-Leaders

Captain Meriwether Lewis

2nd Lieutenant William Clark—Though Clark's captain commission never came through, he was considered and referred to as "captain" by Lewis and all the men throughout the journey.

Sergeants

Charles Floyd—was born in 1782 in Kentucky. He enlisted early, one of the "nine young men from Kentucky." He died on August 1, 1804, near Sioux City, Iowa. Sergeant Floyd was the only man who died on the expedition, presumably of appendicitis.

Patrick Gass—was elected to replace Floyd. A stocky, short, humorous man of Irish descent, he was born on June 12, 1771, in Pennsylvania. After the expedition, he fought in the War of 1812, lost his left eye, and was discharged with a pension. When he was sixty, he married twenty-year-old Maria Hamilton; they had seven children. Gass died in 1870, at age ninety-nine, the last survivor of the expedition. The journal he kept on the expedition was the first to be published. He was noted during the expedition as a woodsman, a boat builder, a fine carpenter, and a good officer.

John Ordway—was born around 1775 in New Hampshire. He died in 1817. An educated man, he holds the distinction of writing in his journal every day of the expedition. This journal was lost for nearly one hundred years after the corps returned. It was found with other Lewis and Clark papers at the American Philosophical Society. Ordway led a group of men when the expedition divided on the homeward trip. When he returned, he bought the land warrants of some of the other men and became a large and prosperous landowner.

Nathaniel Pryor—was born in Amherst County, Virginia, on an unknown date and died in 1831. After the expedition, he remained in the army until 1815, and became a captain. He married an Osage Indian woman and lived in Oklahoma, setting up a trading post on the Arkansas River.

Privates

John Colter—was one of the best hunters and scouts of the expedition. He was born in 1775 in Virginia and grew up in Kentucky. He left the expedition at the Mandan villages to return to the Yellowstone area to trap beaver. Colter discovered Yellowstone while on an exploring trip for fur trader, Manuel Lisa. Colter is remembered mostly for his adventure with the Blackfeet. Captured on a riverbank, he ran naked through a cactus-covered plain, chased by hundreds of warriors. He finally escaped by jumping into the Madison River and hiding under a pile of logs. He then walked for seven days back to Fort Lisa. When he returned from the West, he married, farmed in Missouri, rode with Nathan Boone's rangers, and died, presumably of jaundice, on May 7, 1812.

George Shannon—was just seventeen years old when he joined the expedition. He was valuable as a hunter, a good horseman, and a singer. He was lost several times on the journey, the first time for sixteen days. After the expedition, he served in the army under Pryor, losing his leg after being shot in an Indian conflict. Clark offered him a chance to join the fur trade, but he went to law school instead, becoming a lawyer and eventually a senator from Kentucky.

Other Privates

William Bratton
John Collins
Pierre Cruzatte
Joseph Field
Reubin Field
Robert Frazer
George Gibson
Silas Goodrich
Hugh Hall
Thomas Proctor-Howard
Francis Labiche
Jean Baptiste Lepage
Hugh McNeal
John Potts
John Shields

John B. Thompson
William Werner
Joseph Whitehouse
Alexander Willard
Richard Windsor
Peter Wiser

Soldiers Who Traveled as Far as Fort Mandan

Corporal Richard Warfington
Private John Boley
Private John Dame
Private John Newman
Private Ebenezer Tuttle
Private Isaac White
Private Moses B. Reed (court-martialed and sent
   back to St. Louis)

Civilians

George Drouillard—was the son of a Shawnee Indian
   woman and a French trapper named Pierre
   Drouillard. He was born in Canada and, not as
   lucky as John Colter, was killed at the Three
   Forks by the Blackfeet in 1810. Drouillard was
   an extremely valuable member of the
   expedition. He was the best hunter, calm and
   quick in a crisis, as well as the major
   interpreter from French into English and of
   Indian sign language. After the expedition, he
   bought the land grants of Privates Collins and
   Whitehouse. He returned to the Rocky
   Mountains and was a great help to Clark in
   adding to his topographical information. He

worked for Manuel Lisa before his untimely death.

York—was William Clark's black slave, who became a strong and valuable member of the expedition.

Sacagawea—was the Shoshone Indian woman who accompanied the expedition from the Mandan villages through the return journey. She helped the expedition by pointing out landmarks and sometimes serving as an interpreter.

Toussaint Charbonneau—was the husband of Sacagawea, who served the expedition as an interpreter.

Jean-Baptiste Charbonneau—was the baby born to Sacagawea and Charbonneau during the Lewis and Clark expedition. Called "Pomp" by William Clark, the child accompanied the Corps of Discovery on its journey, and later went to live with William Clark and his family.

★ Chapter Notes ★

Chapter 1. Preparing for Adventure

1. Ingvard Henry Eide, *American Odyssey: The Journey of Lewis and Clark* (Chicago: Rand McNally & Co., 1969), p. 73.

2. Ibid.

3. Bernard DeVoto, ed., *The Journals of Lewis and Clark* (Boston: American Heritage Library, Houghton Mifflin, 1953), p. 134.

Chapter 2. Setting the Stage for the Expedition

1. David Lavender, *The Way to the Western Sea: Lewis and Clark Across the Continent* (New York: Harper & Row, 1988), p. 390.

2. Ibid., p. 392.

3. In Sanford Wexler, *Westward Expansion: An Eyewitness History* (New York: Facts on File, 1991), pp. 52–53.

4. Lavender, p. 55.

5. Judith Edwards, *Colter's Run* (Helena, Mont.: Falcon Press, 1993), p. 20.

6. In Jerome Agel, ed., *Words That Make America Great* (New York: Random House, 1997), p. 81.

7. Bernard DeVoto, ed., *The Journals of Lewis and Clark* (Boston: American Heritage Library, Houghton Mifflin, 1953), pp. 1–3.

8. Ibid., p. 3.

Chapter 3. Running Up the Missouri

1. Bernard DeVoto, ed., *The Journals of Lewis and Clark* (Boston: American Heritage Library, Houghton Mifflin, 1953), p. 17.

2. Robert R. Hunt, "The Blood Meal, Mosquitoes and Agues on the Lewis & Clark Expedition," *We Proceeded On*, vol. 18, no. 2, May 1992, pp. 4–8.

3. DeVoto, p. 14.

4. Ibid., p. 16.

5. Ibid.

6. Stephen E. Ambrose, *Undaunted Courage: Meriwether Lewis, Thomas Jefferson, and the Opening of the American West* (New York: Simon & Schuster, 1966), p. 159.

7. Ingvard Henry Eide, *American Odyssey: The Journey of Lewis and Clark* (Chicago: Rand McNally & Co., 1969), p. 34.

8. DeVoto, p. 24.

9. Interview with present-day Yankton Sioux/Assiniboine medicine man, Wolf Point, Montana, March 15, 1993.

10. Albert and Jane Salisbury, *Lewis and Clark: The Journey West* (New York: Promontory Press, 1993), p. 38.

Chapter 4. Winter at Fort Mandan

1. Bernard DeVoto, ed., *The Journals of Lewis and Clark* (Boston: American Heritage Library, Houghton Mifflin, 1953), p. 74.

2. Stephen E. Ambrose, *Undaunted Courage: Meriwether Lewis, Thomas Jefferson, and the Opening of the American West* (New York: Simon & Schuster, 1996), p. 200.

3. DeVoto, p. 80.

4. Ibid., p. 85.

5. Ibid., p. 92.

Chapter 5. Of Bears and Buffalo

1. Ingvard Henry Eide, *American Odyssey: The Journey of Lewis and Clark* (Chicago: Rand McNally & Co., 1969), p. 52.

2. Ibid.

3. Bernard DeVoto, ed., *The Journals of Lewis and Clark* (Boston: American Heritage Library, Houghton Mifflin, 1953), p. 110.

4. Ibid.

5. Ibid., p. 111.

6. Eide, p. 70.

7. Ibid., p. 65.

8. DeVoto, p. 130.

9. David Lavender, *The Way to the Western Sea: Lewis and Clark Across the Continent* (New York: Harper & Row, 1988), p. 212.

10. DeVoto, pp. 141–142.

11. Ibid., p. 142.

12. Ibid., p. 149.

Chapter 6. Horses and High Mountains Ahead

1. Bernard DeVoto, ed., *The Journals of Lewis and Clark* (Boston: American Heritage Library, Houghton Mifflin, 1953), p. 160.

2. David Lavender, *The Way to the Western Sea: Lewis and Clark Across the Continent* (New York: Harper & Row, 1988), p. 233.

3. Ibid., p. 241.

4. DeVoto, pp. 185–186.

5. Ingvard Henry Eide, *American Odyssey: The Journey of Lewis and Clark* (Chicago: Rand McNally & Co., 1969), p. 91.

6. Ibid., p. 92.

7. Stephen E. Ambrose, *Undaunted Courage: Meriwether Lewis, Thomas Jefferson, and the Opening of the American West* (New York: Simon & Schuster, 1996), p. 266.

8. Ibid., pp. 266–267.

9. Eide, p. 92.

10. DeVoto, p. 206.

Chapter 7. Ocean in View

1. Bernard DeVoto, ed., *The Journals of Lewis and Clark* (Boston: American Heritage Library, Houghton Mifflin, 1953), p. 234.

2. Gary Moulton, ed., *The Journals of the Lewis & Clark Expedition* (Lincoln, Nebr.: University of Nebraska Press, 1989), vol. 5, p. 225.

3. Stephen E. Ambrose, *Undaunted Courage: Meriwether Lewis, Thomas Jefferson, and the Opening of the American West* (New York: Simon & Schuster, 1996), p. 297.

4. DeVoto, p. 279.

Chapter 8. Waiting Out Another Winter

1. In David Colbert, ed., *Eyewitness to America: 500 Years of America in the Words of Those Who Saw It Happen* (New York: Pantheon Books, 1997), p. 112.

2. Stephen E. Ambrose, *Undaunted Courage: Meriwether Lewis, Thomas Jefferson, and the Opening of the American West* (New York: Simon & Schuster, 1996), p. 315.

3. Ingvard Henry Eide, *American Odyssey: The Journey of Lewis and Clark* (Chicago: Rand McNally & Co., 1969), p. 157.

4. Bernard DeVoto, ed., *The Journals of Lewis and Clark* (Boston: American Heritage Library, Houghton Mifflin, 1953), p. 367.

Chapter 9. The Return Trip

1. Bernard DeVoto, ed., *The Journals of Lewis and Clark* (Boston: American Heritage Library, Houghton Mifflin, 1953), p. 440.

2. Gary E. Moulton, ed., *The Journals of the Lewis & Clark Expedition* (Lincoln, Nebr.: University of Nebraska Press, 1993), vol. 8, p. 180.

3. Ibid., p. 372.

Chapter 10. Aftermath and the Trail Today

1. David Lavender, *The Way to the Western Sea: Lewis and Clark Across the Continent* (New York: Harper & Row, 1988), p. 386.

2. Ibid., pp. 384–385.

3. Daniel B. Botkin, *Our Natural History: The Lessons of Lewis and Clark* (New York: G. P. Putnam Sons, 1995), pp. 15–38.

★ FURTHER READING ★

Books

Ambrose, Stephen E. *Undaunted Courage: Meriwether Lewis, Thomas Jefferson, and the Opening of the American West.* New York: Simon & Schuster, 1996.

Botkin, Daniel B. *Our Natural History: The Lessons of Lewis and Clark.* New York: G. P. Putnam Sons, 1995.

DeVoto, Bernard, ed. *The Journals of Lewis and Clark.* Boston: American Heritage Library, Houghton Mifflin, 1953.

Duncan, Dayton. *Out West.* New York: Viking, 1987.

Eide, Ingvard Henry, ed. *American Odyssey: The Journey of Lewis and Clark.* New York: Rand McNally & Co., 1969.

Lavender, David. *The Way to the Western Sea: Lewis and Clark Across the Continent.* New York: Harper & Row, 1988.

Moulton, Gary. *Lewis & Clark & the Route to the Pacific.* Chelsea House, 1991.

Otfinoski, Steven. *Lewis and Clark: Leading America West.* Fawcett Columbine, 1992.

Salisbury, Albert and Jane. *Lewis & Clark: The Journey West.* New York: Promontory Press, 1950.

Streissguth, Tom. *Lewis and Clark: Explorers of the Northwest.* Springfield, N.J.: Enslow Publishers, Inc., 1998.

Internet Addresses

Great Outdoor Recreation Pages. *Lewis and Clark Trail.* n.d. <http://www.gorp.com/gorp/resource/US_TRAIL/LEWIS&CL.HTM> (April 22, 1998).

Lewis and Clark Trail Heritage Foundation. n.d. <http://www.lewisandclark.org/> (April 22, 1998).

VIAs. *Discovering Lewis and Clark.* 1998. <http://www.lewis-clark.org/> (July 24, 1998).

★ INDEX ★